T0064750

Jesus *and* The Disciples Journey

PASTOR REVELLA BOOKER PUGH

WESTBOW
PRESS®
A DIVISION OF THOMAS NELSON
& ZONDERVAN

Copyright © 2020 Pastor Revella Booker Pugh.

All rights reserved. No part of this book may be used or reproduced by any means, graphic, electronic, or mechanical, including photocopying, recording, taping or by any information storage retrieval system without the written permission of the author except in the case of brief quotations embodied in critical articles and reviews.

This book is a work of non-fiction. Unless otherwise noted, the author and the publisher make no explicit guarantees as to the accuracy of the information contained in this book and in some cases, names of people and places have been altered to protect their privacy.

WestBow Press books may be ordered through booksellers or by contacting:

WestBow Press
A Division of Thomas Nelson & Zondervan
1663 Liberty Drive
Bloomington, IN 47403
www.westbowpress.com
1 (866) 928-1240

Because of the dynamic nature of the Internet, any web addresses or links contained in this book may have changed since publication and may no longer be valid. The views expressed in this work are solely those of the author and do not necessarily reflect the views of the publisher, and the publisher hereby disclaims any responsibility for them.

Any people depicted in stock imagery provided by Getty Images are models, and such images are being used for illustrative purposes only.
Certain stock imagery © Getty Images.

Scripture quotations taken from the King James Version of the Bible.

ISBN: 978-1-9736-9529-5 (sc)
ISBN: 978-1-9736-9531-8 (hc)
ISBN: 978-1-9736-9530-1 (e)

Library of Congress Control Number: 2020911892

Print information available on the last page.

WestBow Press rev. date: 9/22/2020

My Most Sincere Appreciation

I would like to thank my daughter, Bethany, a Harvard College graduate, for the awesome contribution and participation in assisting with the writing of this book.

Bethany's academic experience, patience, detailed observation, and editing of this book made the process much easier to complete than anticipated.

Thank you, Bethany. You are an asset.

CONTENTS

ACKNOWLEDGEMENTS

I begin in thanking GOD for the encouragement, confidence and the ability to write this book and never allowing me to doubt, waver or loose faith as I was writing it.

I also must thank GOD'S ANONTED HOUSE TRUSTEES, Bethany Lynne Pugh, Kathleen Miles, Walter Holman, Brenda Gradford and Rose Aubourg for the support and prayers as I was writing my book.

I would also like to thank the community where I live, Highland Heights, Oh. Though they were a silent majority, their silence and their encouragement are much appreciated.

INTRODUCTION

It is very important for you, as a disciple of Jesus Christ, whether you are an experienced follower of Jesus or just starting your journey as a new follower of Jesus, to gain as much knowledge as you can as you grow and mature into being the disciple God would have you be.

"What is a disciple?

A follower, an adherent to the doctrines of another. Christ's disciples were followers of His doctrines. "[1]

Therefore, we as Christians are also Christ disciples and followers of the doctrines of Christ and His disciples.

"What are doctrines?

In a general sense, whatever is taught. A principle or position in any science; whatever is laid down as true by an instructor or master. The doctrines of the gospel are the principles or truths taught by Christ and His apostles."[2]

What was the apostles doctrine? Jesus says in John 7:16–17, "My doctrine is not mine, but HIS that sent me. If any man will do HIS will, he shall know of the doctrine, whether it be of God, or whether I speak of myself."

The apostle doctrines were their teachings:

---

[1] Website ©2020 AV1611.com King James Dictionary
[2] Website ©2020 AV1611.com King James Dictionary

There is only one God
Water baptism
Tongues
Holiness
Divine healing
Second coming of Christ
Resurrection
Judgment

Jesus is the one we are to follow at all times. He is the ultimate disciple. However, you must take heed to the other disciples as well, because as you shall see, they followed Jesus faithfully, awesomely, and with loyalty.

CHAPTER 1

The Beginning of Jesus's Ministry

Scripture: Mark 1:1-45

"Jesus Christ

Birth: Between 6–4 BC

Conceived by the Holy Spirit, birthed by a virgin named Mary

Heavenly Father: God

Earthly father: Joseph

Brothers and sisters: "Is not this the carpenter, the son of Mary, the brother of James, and Joses, Joseph and of Juda, and Simon? and are not his sisters here with us? And they were offended at him" (Mark 6:3). Jesus had sisters, but it does not mention their names.

Death: Between AD 30-36" [1]

Resurrection: Three days after his death

We shall begin with the genealogy of Jesus because it is important to know as a disciple of Jesus Chrisst

Although genealogies are good to have knowledge of, we are not to seek it in an obsessive way because scripture says in 1 Timothy 1:4, "Neither give heed to fables and endless genealogies, which minister questions, rather than godly edifying which is in faith: so do."

The book of the generation of Jesus Christ, the son of David, the son of Abraham.

Abraham begat Isaac; and Isaac begat Jacob; and Jacob begat Judas and his brethren;

And Judas begat Phares and Zara of Thamar; and Phares begat Esrom; and Esrom begat Aram;

And Aram begat Aminadab; and Aminadab begat Naasson; and Naasson begat Salmon;

And Salmon begat Booz of Rachab; and Booz begat Obed of Ruth; and Obed begat Jesse;

And Jesse begat David the king; and David the king begat Solomon of her that had been the wife of Urias;

And Solomon begat Roboam; and Roboam begat Abia; and Abia begat Asa;

And Asa begat Josaphat; and Josaphat begat Joram; and Joram begat Ozias;

And Ozias begat Joatham; and Joatham begat Achaz; and Achaz begat Ezekias;

And Ezekias begat Manasses; and Manasses begat Amon; and Amon begat Josias;

And Josias begat Jechonias and his brethren, about the time they were carried away to Babylon:

And after they were brought to Babylon, Jechonias begat Salathiel; and Salathiel begat Zorobabel;

And Zorobabel begat Abiud; and Abiud begat Eliakim; and Eliakim begat Azor;

And Azor begat Sadoc; and Sadoc begat Achim; and Achim begat Eliud;

And Eliud begat Eleazar; and Eleazar begat Matthan; and Matthan begat Jacob;

And Jacob begat Joseph the husband of Mary, of whom was born Jesus, who is called Christ.

So all the generations from Abraham to David are fourteen generations; and from David until the carrying away into Babylon are fourteen generations; and from the carrying away into Babylon unto Christ are fourteen generations. (Matthew 1:1–17)

Jesus's genealogy is beneficial in order to know whom he came from. We are now going into the birth, ministry, crucifixion, resurrection, and ascension of Jesus as a disciple while on this earth.

The Birth of Jesus

Jesus was born in a stable in Bethlehem because there was no room in the inn. This was the most humble place in which a person could be born. Jesus was wrapped in swaddling clothes, lying in a manger where Mary and Joseph, Jesus's mother and earthly father, were present, and in Luke Chapter 2 it describes the shepherds at the time they came to Jesus right after his birth.

They were watching their flock by night, and came and beheld His presence.

> And it came to pass in those days, that there went out a decree from Caesar Augustus that all the world should be taxed.

> (And this taxing was first made when Cyrenius was governor of Syria.)

> And all went to be taxed, every one into his own city.

> And Joseph also went up from Galilee, out of the city of Nazareth, into Judaea, unto the city of David, which is called Bethlehem; (because he was of the house and lineage of David:)

> To be taxed with Mary his espoused wife, being great with child.

> And so it was, that, while they were there, the days were accomplished that she should be delivered.

> And she brought forth her firstborn son, and wrapped him in swaddling clothes, and laid him in a manger; because there was no room for them in the inn.

> And there were in the same country shepherds abiding in the field, keeping watch over their flock by night

And, lo, the angel of the Lord came upon them, and the glory of the Lord shone round about them: and they were sore afraid.

And the angel said unto them, Fear not: for, behold, I bring you good tidings of great joy, which shall be to all people.

For unto you is born this day in the city of David a Saviour, which is Christ the Lord.

And this shall be a sign unto you; Ye shall find the babe wrapped in swaddling clothes, lying in a manger.

And suddenly there was with the angel a multitude of the heavenly host praising God, and saying,

Glory to God in the highest, and on earth peace, good will toward men.

And it came to pass, as the angels were gone away from them into heaven, the shepherds said one to another, Let us now go even unto Bethlehem, and see this thing which is come to pass, which the Lord hath made known unto us.

And they came with haste, and found Mary, and Joseph, and the babe lying in a manger.

And when they had seen it, they made known abroad the saying which was told them concerning this child. (Luke 2:1–17)

However, there is a clear distinction between the shepherds being present at Jesus birth, of which was just mentioned, and the wise men being present years after Jesus birth.

The wise men visitation of Jesus came after Jesus and was near two years old. "Matthew tells of their visitation and the gifts of gold, frankincense and myrrh they brought to Jesus.

> Now when Jesus was born in Bethlehem of Judaea in the days of Herod the king, behold, there came wise men from the east to Jerusalem,
>
> Saying, Where is he that is born King of the Jews? for we have seen his star in the east, and are come to worship him.
>
> When Herod the king had heard these things, he was troubled, and all Jerusalem with him.
>
> And when he had gathered all the chief priests and scribes of the people together, he demanded of them where Christ should be born.
>
> And they said unto him, In Bethlehem of Judaea: for thus it is written by the prophet,
>
> And thou Bethlehem, in the land of Juda, art not the least among the princes of Juda: for out of thee shall come a Governor, that shall rule my people Israel.
>
> Then Herod, when he had privily called the wise men, enquired of them diligently what time the star appeared.
>
> And he sent them to Bethlehem, and said, Go and search diligently for the young child; and when ye have found him, bring me word again, that I may come and worship him also.
>
> When they had heard the king, they departed; and, lo, the star, which they saw in the east, went before them, till it came and stood over where the young child was.

When they saw the star, they rejoiced with exceeding great joy.

And when they were come into the house, they saw the young child (not a baby but a young child) with Mary his mother, and fell down, and worshipped him: and when they had opened their treasures, they presented unto him gifts; gold, and frankincense and myrrh. (Matthew 2:1–11)

It was proven that Jesus was a king when the wise men brought him gold (which represents Jesus as the Divine King), frankincense (which represents Jesus as the High Priest), and myrrh (for burial, representing the suffering and death Jesus would have to endure)."[1]

---

[1] en.wikipedia.org Biblical Magi – Wikipedia

Jesus's Miracles during His Ministry

Jesus's ministry began when He was thirty years old. It culminated when He was thirty-three years old. Three years for such an awesome ministry. But what Jesus did in those three years, not one person has done in a lifetime.

The very beginning of Jesus's ministry was after John the Baptist baptized Him in the Jordan River.

I would like to interject this thought. Jesus was baptized first, before His ministry began. I have heard some people say that baptism is not essential to salvation.

However, as disciples of Jesus, we are to follow Jesus in obedience as Jesus followed God so we can do the works Jesus did and even more. Jesus was baptized, and as an act of obedience, you should be baptized as well.

Now after Jesus was baptized, He departed from there and began to fast for forty days and forty nights in the wilderness.

During your discipleship, you too are going to experience some time in the wilderness. There will be time where God wants you to be alone with Him so He can give you revelations, inspiration, and motivation to continue to build the foundation for you to stay on. That foundation is the straight and narrow pathway.

During Jesus's time in the wilderness, He was tempted by the devil, who thought Jesus was in such a weak state that He would worship him as opposed to God.

However, Jesus overcame any and all temptations from the devil because when you fast and pray, it might weaken you in the natural, but it strengthens you in the spiritual.

After Jesus left the wilderness, He began doing His miracles, signs, and wonders, which allowed Him to save many souls for the kingdom.

Moreover, all things are possible with God. Yes, even today, we as the body of Christ should not only be performing these miracles, signs, and wonders that Jesus performed, but we should be doing even greater works. As John 14:12 says, "Verily, verily, I say unto you, He that believeth on me, the works that I do shall he do also; and greater works than these shall he do; because I go unto my Father."

Jesus performed many miracles, signs, and wonders during his journey on this earth, and listed below are all of his "miracles, signs, and wonders He performed with scripture notated."[1]

It might seem overwhelming to do even greater works, but remember all things are possible with God.

Miracles, Signs, and Wonders	Matthew	Mark	Luke	John
Healing the mother of Peter's wife	8:14–15	1:29–31	4:38–41	
Healing the blind at Birth				9:1–41
Healing the paralytic at Bethesda				5:1–16
Healing the blind man at Bethsaida		8:22–36		
Healing the blind man Bartimaeus in Jericho		10:46–52		
Healing the centurion's servant	8:5–13		7:1–10	

---

[1] https://en.wikipedia.org/wiki/Miracles_of_Jesus
Miracles of Jesus – Wikipedia

Healing an infirm woman			13:10–17	
The man with a withered hand	12:9–13	3:1–6	6:6–11	
Cleansing a leper	8:1–4	1:40–45	5:12–16	
Healing a man with dropsy			14:1–6	
Healing a bleeding woman	9:20–22	5:25–34	8:43–48	
Healing the paralytic at Capernaum	9:1–8	2:1–12	5:17–26	
Healing in Gennesaret		6:53–56		
Healing a boy possessed by a demon		9:14–29		
Healing the Canaanite woman's daughter	15:21–28	7:24–30		
Healing the Gerasenes demonic	8:28–34	5:1–20	8:26–39	
Healing a deaf man		7:31–37		
Healing Jairus's daughter	9:18–26	5:21–43	8:40–56	
Raising Lazarus from the dead				11:1–44
Turning water into wine				2:1–11
Walking on water	14:22–34	6:45–53		6:15–21
Transfiguration	17:1–8	9:2–8	9:28–36	

Feeding the multitude (4,000 and 5,000)	14:13–21 15:32–39	6:31–44 8:1–9	9:12–17	6:1–14
Draught of fishes			5:1–11	21:1–14
Coin in the fishes mouth	17:24–27			
Calming the storm	8:23–27	4:35–41	8:22–25	

Jesus's Travels

"Decapolis was comprised of an alliance of ten cities, originally Palestinian. All but one (Scythopolis) was on the east side of the Jordan. In New Testament times these cities were most definitely Greek in character and under the protection of Rome (Governor of Syria).

1. Gerasa in Jordan
2. Scythopolis, in Israel, the only city west of the Jordan River
3. Hippos, on the Golden Heights
4. Gadara, in Jordan
5. Pella, in Jordan
6. Philadelphia, modern-day Amman, the capital of Jordan
7. Capitolias, in Jordan
8. Canatha in Syria
9. Paphaa in Jordan
10. Damascus, capital of modern Syria

Source: en.wikipedia.org wiki Decapolis1

Scriptures on Jesus's Travel to Decapolis

> And again, departing from the coasts of Tyre and Sidon,
> HE came unto the Sea of Galilee, through the midst of
> the coasts of Decapolis. (Mark 7:31)

The New Testament gospels of Matthew, Mark, and Luke mention that
the Decapolis region was a location of the ministry of Jesus. The Decapolis
was one of the few regions where Jesus traveled in which Gentiles (people
who are not Jewish) were in the majority.

Mark 5:1–20 emphasizes the Decapolis's Gentile character when Jesus
encounters a herd of pigs.

> And they came over unto the other side of the sea, into
> the country of the Gadarenes.
>
> And when he was come out of the ship, immediately there
> met him out of the tombs a man with an unclean spirit,
>
> Who had his dwelling among the tombs; and no man
> could bind him, no, not with chains:
>
> Because that he had been often bound with fetters and
> chains, and the chains had been plucked asunder by him,
> and the fetters broken in pieces: neither could any man
> tame him.
>
> And always, night and day, he was in the mountains, and
> in the tombs, crying, and cutting himself with stones.
>
> But when he saw Jesus afar off, he ran and worshipped him,
>
> And cried with a loud voice, and said, What have I to do
> with thee, Jesus, thou Son of the most high God? I adjure
> thee by God, that thou torment me not.

For he said unto him, Come out of the man, thou unclean spirit.

And he asked him, What is thy name? And he answered, saying, My name is Legion: for we are many.

And he besought him much that he would not send them away out of the country.

Now there was there nigh unto the mountains a great herd of swine feeding.

And all the devils besought him, saying, Send us into the swine, that we may enter into them.

And forthwith Jesus gave them leave. And the unclean spirits went out, and entered into the swine: and the herd ran violently down a steep place into the sea, (they were about two thousand) and were choked in the sea.

And they that fed the swine fled, and told it in the city, and in the country. And they went out to see what it was that was done.[1]

And they come to Jesus, and see him that was possessed with the devil, and had the legion, sitting, and clothed, and in his right mind: and they were afraid.

And they that saw it told them how it befell to him that was possessed with the devil, and also concerning the swine.

And they began to pray him to depart out of their coasts.

And when he was come into the ship, he that had been possessed with the devil prayed him that he might be with him.

Howbeit Jesus suffered him not, but saith unto him, Go home to thy friends, and tell them how great things the Lord hath done for thee, and hath had compassion on thee.

And he departed, and began to publish in Decapolis how great things Jesus had done for him: and all men did marvel.

Life and Ministry of, Jesus

"Born to the Virgin Mary—Luke 1, 2
Simeon and Anna recognize Messiah—Luke 2
Flight to Egypt—Matthew 2
Jesus's childhood home—Matthew 2
Jesus confounds doctors of the law—Luke 2
Jesus's baptism by John the Baptist—John 1
Tempted by Satan in the wilderness—Luke 4
Turns water in wine at Cana wedding—John 2
Jesus cleanses the temple for the first time, talks with Nicodemus—John 2, 3
Woman at Jacob's well—John 4
Heals official's son—John 4
Jesus rejected in hometown—Luke 4
Jesus lives here during ministry—Matthew 4
Jesus heals cripple at pool—John 5
Appoints the twelve apostles, Sermon on the Mount—Luke 6, Matthew 5–7
John the Baptist is killed by Herod—Mark 6
Miracle of feeding 5,000—John 6
Jesus walks on water—Matthew 14
Jesus performs many miracles—Mark 6
Jesus preaches he is the bread of life—John 6
Women asks for daughter to be healed—Mark 7
Miraculous feeding of 4,000—Mark 8
Jews demand Jesus show them a sign to prove He is the Messiah—Mark 8
Jesus heals man from Bethsaida who is blind—Mark 8
Peter says Jesus is the Messiah—Luke 9
The transfiguration—Luke 9
Jesus cleanse ten lepers—Luke 17
Jesus, at the pool of Siloam, heals man who was born blind—John 9
Jesus raises Lazarus from the dead—John 11 "[1]

---

[1] Source: www.biblestudy.org

CHAPTER 2

Jesus Calls His First Disciples as Told in Matthew, Mark, Luke, and John

Matthew 4:18–22 gives the order in which the disciples were called.

> And Jesus, walking by the sea of Galilee, saw two brethren, Simon called Peter, and Andrew his brother, casting a net into the sea: for they were fishers.
>
> And he saith unto them, Follow me, and I will make you fishers of men.
>
> And they straightway left their nets, and followed him.
>
> And going on from thence, he saw other two brethren, James the son of Zebedee, and John his brother, in a ship with Zebedee their father, mending their nets; and he called them.
>
> And they immediately left the ship and their father, and followed him. Simon Peter, Andrew, James, son of Zebedee and his brother John.

Mark 1:16–20 tells the same story as Matthew 4:18–22.

> Now as he walked by the sea of Galilee, he saw Simon and Andrew his brother casting a net into the sea: for they were fishers.
>
> And Jesus said unto them, Come ye after me, and I will make you to become fishers of men.
>
> And straightway they forsook their nets, and followed him.
>
> And when he had gone a little farther thence, he saw James the son of Zebedee, and John his brother, who also were in the ship mending their nets.
>
> And straightway he called them: and they left their father Zebedee in the ship with the hired servants, and went after him.

Simon Peter and Andrew; James, the son of Zebedee; and his brother John

Luke 5:1–11 states,

> And it came to pass, that, as the people pressed upon him to hear the word of God, he stood by the lake of Gennesaret,
>
> And saw two ships standing by the lake: but the fishermen were gone out of them, and were washing their nets.
>
> And he entered into one of the ships, which was Simon's, and prayed him that he would thrust out a little from the land. And he sat down, and taught the people out of the ship.
>
> Now when he had left speaking, he said unto Simon, Launch out into the deep, and let down your nets for a draught.

And Simon answering said unto him, Master, we have toiled all the night, and have taken nothing: nevertheless at thy word I will let down the net.

And when they had this done, they inclosed a great multitude of fishes: and their net brake.

And they beckoned unto their partners, which were in the other ship, that they should come and help them. And they came, and filled both the ships, so that they began to sink.

When Simon Peter saw it, he fell down at Jesus' knees, saying, Depart from me; for I am a sinful man, O Lord.

For he was astonished, and all that were with him, at the draught of the fishes which they had taken:

And so was also James, and John, the sons of Zebedee, which were partners with Simon. And Jesus said unto Simon, Fear not; from henceforth thou shalt catch men.

And when they had brought their ships to land, they forsook all, and followed him.

John 1:35–51

Again the next day after John stood, and two of his disciples;

And looking upon Jesus as he walked, he saith, Behold the Lamb of God!

And the two disciples heard him speak, and they followed Jesus.

Then Jesus turned, and saw them following, and saith unto them, What seek ye? They said unto him, Rabbi, (which is to say, being interpreted, Master,) where dwellest thou?

He saith unto them, Come and see. They came and saw where he dwelt, and abode with him that day: for it was about the tenth hour.

One of the two which heard John speak, and followed him, was Andrew, Simon Peter's brother.

He first findeth his own brother Simon, and saith unto him, We have found the Messias, which is, being interpreted, the Christ.

And he brought him to Jesus. And when Jesus beheld him, he said, Thou art Simon the son of Jona: thou shalt be called Cephas, which is by interpretation, A stone.

The day following Jesus would go forth into Galilee, and findeth Philip, and saith unto him, Follow me.

Now Philip was of Bethsaida, the city of Andrew and Peter.

Philip findeth Nathanael, and saith unto him, We have found him, of whom Moses in the law, and the prophets, did write, Jesus of Nazareth, the son of Joseph.

And Nathanael said unto him, Can there any good thing come out of Nazareth? Philip saith unto him, Come and see.

Jesus saw Nathanael coming to him, and saith of him, Behold an Israelite indeed, in whom is no guile!

Nathanael saith unto him, Whence knowest thou me? Jesus answered and said unto him, Before that Philip called thee, when thou wast under the fig tree, I saw thee.

Nathanael answered and saith unto him, Rabbi, thou art the Son of God; thou art the King of Israel.

Jesus answered and said unto him, Because I said unto thee, I saw thee under the fig tree, believest thou? thou shalt see greater things than these.

And he saith unto him, Verily, verily, I say unto you, Hereafter ye shall see heaven open, and the angels of God ascending and descending upon the Son of man.

Andrew and Simon (Peter), his brother (whom Jesus called Cephas, the stone), Philip and Nathanael (can anything good come out Nazareth)

Jesus Calls All of His Disciples

Matthew 10:1–4 states,

> And when he had called unto him his twelve disciples, he gave them power against unclean spirits, to cast them out, and to heal all manner of sickness and all manner of disease.
>
> Now the names of the twelve apostles are these; The first, Simon, who is called Peter, and Andrew his brother; James the son of Zebedee, and John his brother;
>
> Philip, and Bartholomew; Thomas, and Matthew the publican; James the son of Alphaeus, and Lebbaeus, whose surname was Thaddaeus;
>
> Simon the Canaanite, and Judas Iscariot, who also betrayed him.

Andrew
Bartholomew or Nathanael
James, the Elder
James, the Lesser or Younger
John
Judas
Jude or Thaddeus
Matthew or Levi
Peter or (Simon Peter)
Philip
Simon the Zealot
Thomas, doubting

The Disciples and Their Works

Each disciple and his works should enlighten you more into following after Jesus until you have learned to decrease and let God increase in your discipleship journey. Their works should awaken you into knowing, believing, and accepting the discipleship calling upon your life.

Andrew

"The name Andrew is Greek and means "manly, brave, from manhood, valor.

> Birthdate: Early first century
> Place of Birth: Bethsaida on the Sea of Galilee, Roman Empire
> Year of Birth: Circa AD 5
> Parents: Son of Jona
> Occupation: Fisherman
> Death: Mid to late first century, Patras, Achaia, Roman Empire (sixty-five years old)"[1]

Andrew brought his brother, Peter, to Jesus (John 1:40–41). "At the beginning of Jesus's public life, it was said Andrew and Jesus occupied the same house at Capernaum.

Many scholars say that Andrew preached in Scythia, Greece, and Asia Minor.

In Matthew 4:18–22 and in Mark 1:16–20, Simon Peter and Andrew were both called together to become disciples of Jesus and "fishers of men." These narratives record that Jesus was walking along the shore of the Sea of Galilee, observed Simon and Andrew fishing, and called them to discipleship.

Subsequently in the Gospels, Andrew is referred to as being present on some important occasions as one of the disciples more closely attached to Jesus. Andrew told Jesus about the boy with the loaves and fishes (John 6:8–9), and when Philip wanted to tell Jesus about certain Greeks seeking Him, he told Andrew first (John 12:20–22). Andrew was present at the Last Supper.

---

[1] Source: https://en.wikipedia.org/wiki/Andrew_the_Apostle

Andrew introduced others to Jesus. Although circumstances placed him in a position where it would have been easy for him to become jealous and resentful, he was optimistic and well content as a follower of Jesus. His main purpose in life was to bring others to the Master, as is ours today.

According to tradition, it was in Achaia, Greece, in the town of Patra, that Andrew died a martyr. Governor Aepeas's wife was healed and converted to the Christian faith, and shortly after that, the governor's brother became a Christian. Aepeas was enraged. He arrested Andrew and condemned him to die on the cross.

Andrew, feeling unworthy to be crucified on the same-shaped cross as his Master, begged that his be different. He was crucified on an X-shaped cross, which is still called Saint Andrew's cross and which is one of his apostolic symbols. A symbol of two crossed fish has also been applied to Andrew because he was formerly a fisherman."[2]

Andrew was originally a disciple of John the Baptist (John 1:40).

[2] : https://en.wikipedia.org/wiki/Andrew_the_Apostle

"Bartholomew or Possibly Nathaneal

The name means "son of Tolmai or Talmai" (2 Samuel 3:3), or son of the furrows (perhaps a ploughman).

> Birthdate: 1st century AD
> Place of Birth: Cana of Galilee
> Death: 1st Century AD"[1]

"Bartholomew's apostolic symbol is three parallel knives. Tradition says he was a missionary in Armenia. A number of scholars believe that he was the only one of the twelve disciples who came from royal blood or noble birth. Talmai was king of Geshur, and his daughter, Maacah, was the wife of David, mother of Absolom."[2]

Bartholomew's name appears with these lists of the disciples.

> Philip, and Bartholomew; Thomas, and Matthew the publican; James the son of Alphaeus, and Lebbaeus, whose surname was Thaddaeus. (Matthew 10:3)

> And Andrew, and Philip, and Bartholomew, and Matthew, and Thomas, and James the son of Alphaeus, and Thaddaeus, and Simon the Canaanite. (Mark 3:18)

> And when it was day, he called unto him his disciples: and of them he chose twelve, whom also he named apostles; Simon, (whom he also named Peter), and Andrew his brother, James and John, Philip and Bartholomew, Matthew and Thomas, James the son of Alphaeus, and Simon called Zelotes, And Judas the brother of James, and Judas Iscariot, which also was the traitor. (Luke 6:13–16)

---

[1] Source: https://en.wikipedia.org/wiki/Bartholomew_the_Apostle
[2] : https://en.wikipedia.org/wiki/Bartholomew_the_Apostle

And when they were come in, they went up into an upper room, where abode both Peter, and James, and John, and Andrew, Philip, and Thomas, Bartholomew, and Matthew, James the son of Alphaeus, and Simon Zelotes, and Judas the brother of James. (Acts 1:13)

"The New Testament gives us very little information about Bartholomew. Tradition indicates he was a great searcher of the Scripture and a scholar in the law and the prophets. He developed into a man of complete surrender to the Carpenter of Nazareth, and he was one of the Church's most adventurous missionaries. He is said to have preached with Philip in Phrygia and Hierapolis, as well as in Armenia. The Armenian Church claims him as its founder and martyr. However, tradition says that he preached in India, and his death seems to have taken place there. He died as a martyr for his Lord. He was flayed alive with knives.

In the Gospel of John, Nathanael is introduced as a friend of Philip, from Bethsaida. The first disciples called by Jesus are all portrayed as reaching out immediately to family or friends; thus, Philip found Nathanael and said to him, "We have found Him of whom Moses in the law, and also the prophets, wrote—Jesus of Nazareth, the son of Joseph" (John 1:45).

Nathanael is described as initially being skeptical about whether the Messiah could come from Nazareth, saying, "Can anything good come out of Nazareth" (John 1:46). Nonetheless, he accepts Philip's invitation to find out.

Jesus immediately characterizes him as "an Israelite in whom is no deceit" (John 1:47). Some scholars hold that Jesus's quote, "Before Philip called you, when you were under the fig tree, I saw you," is based on a Jewish figure of speech, referring to studying the Torah. Nathanael recognizes Jesus as "the Son of God" and "the King of Israel" (John 1:49).

He reappears (as Nathanael of Cana) at the end of John's Gospel, as one of the disciples to whom Jesus appeared at the Sea of Galilee after the Resurrection (John 21:1–2).

Nathanael has often been identified with Bartholomew, the apostle mentioned in the Synoptic Gospels, although most modern commentators reject the identification of Nathanael with Bartholomew.

Christian tradition has three stories about Bartholomew's death.

1. One speaks of his being kidnapped, beaten unconscious, and cast into the sea to drown.
2. Another account states that he was crucified upside down.
3. Another says that he was skinned alive and beheaded in Albac or Albanopolis, near Başkale, Turkey.

The account of Bartholomew being skinned alive is the most represented in works of art, and consequently Bartholomew is often shown with a large knife holding his own skin."[3]

---

[3] : https://en.wikipedia.org/wiki/Bartholomew_the_Apostle

James the Elder, the Greater, the Great

> "Birthdate: Not Available
> Place of Birth: Bethsaida, Judaea, Roman Empire
> Parents: Son of Zebedee and Salome
> Siblings: John the Apostle
> Death: 44 AD, Jerusalem, Judaea, Roman Empire"[1]

"James, son of Zebedee, was traditionally considered the first apostle to be martyred in Acts 12:1–2 because of his faith. He was a son of Zebedee and Salome and the brother of John the Apostle. He is also called James the Greater or James the Great, to distinguish him from James, son of Alphaeus, and James, the brother of Jesus (James the Just).

James is described as one of the first disciples to join Jesus (Mark 1:19–20). The Synoptic Gospels state that James and John were with their father by the seashore when Jesus called them to follow Him. James was one of only three apostles whom Jesus selected to bear witness to His transfiguration (Luke 9:28–31), the raising of the daughter of Jairus from the dead (Mark 5:37–43), and Jesus's agony in the Garden of Gethsemane (Matthew 26:36–37).

James and John (or, in another tradition, their mother) asked Jesus to grant them seats on his right and left in His glory. Jesus rebuked them, and the other ten apostles were annoyed with them.

James and his younger brother, the apostle St. John, are designated Boanerges (from the Greek boanerges), or "sons of thunder."

> And James the son of Zebedee, and John the brother of James; and he surnamed them Boanerges, which is, The sons of thunder, (Mark 3:17)

Perhaps it was because of their characteristic fiery zeal.

---

[1] Source: en.wikipedia.org, James the Great – Wikipedia

And when his disciples James and John saw this, they said,
Lord, wilt thou that we command fire to come down from
heaven, and consume them, even as Elias did? (Luke 9:54)

With Peter and Andrew, James and John were the first four disciples
whom Jesus called (Mark 1:16–19) and whose question ("Tell us, when
will this [the end of time] be, and what will be the sign when these things
are all to be accomplished?") sparks Jesus's eschatological discourse in
Mark 13."

Merriam-Webster's Dictionary defines *eschatological* as follows.

1. a branch of theology concerned with the final events in the history
    of the world or of humankind
2. a belief concerning death, the end of the world, or the ultimate
    destiny of humankind;

> And as he went out of the temple, one of his disciples saith
> unto him, Master, see what manner of stones and what
> buildings are here!
>
> And Jesus answering said unto him, Seest thou these great
> buildings? there shall not be left one stone upon another,
> that shall not be thrown down.
>
> And as he sat upon the mount of Olives over against the
> temple, Peter and James and John and Andrew asked him
> privately,
>
> Tell us, when shall these things be? and what shall be the
> sign when all these things shall be fulfilled?
>
> And Jesus answering them began to say, Take heed lest
> any man deceive you:

For many shall come in my name, saying, I am Christ; and shall deceive many.

And when ye shall hear of wars and rumours of wars, be ye not troubled: for such things must needs be; but the end shall not be yet.

For nation shall rise against nation, and kingdom against kingdom: and there shall be earthquakes in divers places, and there shall be famines and troubles: these are the beginnings of sorrows.

But take heed to yourselves: for they shall deliver you up to councils; and in the synagogues ye shall be beaten: and ye shall be brought before rulers and kings for my sake, for a testimony against them.

And the gospel must first be published among all nations.

But when they shall lead you, and deliver you up, take no thought beforehand what ye shall speak, neither do ye premeditate: but whatsoever shall be given you in that hour, that speak ye: for it is not ye that speak, but the Holy Ghost.

Now the brother shall betray the brother to death, and the father the son; and children shall rise up against their parents, and shall cause them to be put to death.

And ye shall be hated of all men for my name's sake: but he that shall endure unto the end, the same shall be saved.

But when ye shall see the abomination of desolation, spoken of by Daniel the prophet, standing where it ought not, (let him that readeth understand,) then let them that be in Judaea flee to the mountains:

And let him that is on the housetop not go down into the house, neither enter therein, to take any thing out of his house:

And let him that is in the field not turn back again for to take up his garment.

But woe to them that are with child, and to them that give suck in those days!

And pray ye that your flight be not in the winter.

For in those days shall be affliction, such as was not from the beginning of the creation which God created unto this time, neither shall be.

And except that the Lord had shortened those days, no flesh should be saved: but for the elect's sake, whom he hath chosen, he hath shortened the days.

And then if any man shall say to you, Lo, here is Christ; or, lo, he is there; believe him not:

For false christs and false prophets shall rise, and shall shew signs and wonders, to seduce, if it were possible, even the elect.

But take ye heed: behold, I have foretold you all things.

But in those days, after that tribulation, the sun shall be darkened, and the moon shall not give her light,

And the stars of heaven shall fall, and the powers that are in heaven shall be shaken.

And then shall they see the Son of man coming in the clouds with great power and glory.

And then shall he send his angels, and shall gather together his elect from the four winds, from the uttermost part of the earth to the uttermost part of heaven.

Now learn a parable of the fig tree; When her branch is yet tender, and putteth forth leaves, ye know that summer is near:

So ye in like manner, when ye shall see these things come to pass, know that it is nigh, even at the doors.

Verily I say unto you, that this generation shall not pass, till all these things be done.

Heaven and earth shall pass away: but my words shall not pass away.

But of that day and that hour knoweth no man, no, not the angels which are in heaven, neither the Son, but the Father.

Take ye heed, watch and pray: for ye know not when the time is.

For the Son of Man is as a man taking a far journey, who left his house, and gave authority to his servants, and to every man his work, and commanded the porter to watch.

Watch ye therefore: for ye know not when the master of the house cometh, at even, or at midnight, or at the cockcrowing, or in the morning:

Lest coming suddenly he find you sleeping.

And what I say unto you I say unto all, Watch. (Mark 13:1–37)

"As a member of the inner circle, James witnessed the raising of Jairus's daughter (Mark 5:37; Luke 8:51), the transfiguration (Mark 9:2), and Jesus's agony in the Garden of Gethsemane (Mark 14:33; Matthew 26:37). James and John asked Jesus to let them sit, one at His right and one at His left, in His future glory (Mark 10:35–40)—a favor that Jesus said was not His to grant. :"[2]

---

[2] **britanica.com Saint James APOSTLE, SON OF ZEBEDEE**
(WRITTEN BY: The Editors of Encyclopaedia Britannica)
(LAST UPDATED: Jan 1, 2020 See Article History)

James, the Lesser or Younger

> "Birthdate: Unknown
> Place of Birth: Galilee, Israel
> Parents: Alphaes Cleophas, Mary
> Siblings: Matthew the Apostle, Jude the Apostle
> Death: 62 or 69 AD, Ostrakine"[1]

James the Less is a figure of early Christianity, one of the Twelve chosen by Jesus. He is also called "the Minor", "the Little", "the Lesser", or "the Younger", according to translation. He is not to be confused with James, son of Zebedee ("James the Great or Elder"). In the West he was for long (and still is) identified with James, the Lord's brother, thought of by St Jerome and those who followed him as really the cousin of Jesus. The sources offer no certainty. Most New Testament scholars now would reject that identification of St James the Less (one of the Twelve, though a fairly insignificant member) with St James, an actual brother of Jesus, and leader of the early Christian Jewish community. As a result, while St James the Less continues to be commemorated with St Philip on May 1st in the Western calendars, increasingly St James the Brother of the Lord has been included in those Calendars."[1]

"At some time in the forty days that intervened between the resurrection and the ascension the Lord appeared to him. (1 Corinthians 15:7) Ten years after we find James on a level with Peter, and with him deciding on the admission of St. Paul into fellowship with the Church at Jerusalem; and from henceforth we always find him equal, or in his own department superior, to the very chiefest apostles, Peter, John and Paul. (Acts 9:27; Galatians 1:18,19) This pre-eminence is evident throughout the after history of the apostles, whether we read it in the Acts, in the epistles or in ecclesiastical writers. (Acts 12:17; 15:13,19; 21:18; Galatians 2:9) According to tradition, James was thrown down from the temple by the scribes and Pharisees; he was then stoned, and his brains dashed out with a fuller's club."[2]

---

[1] Source: ://en.wikipedia.org/wiki/
[2] biblehub.com, Smith's Bible Dictionary James the Less

John

> "Birthdate: AD 6
> Place of Birth: Bethsaida, Galilee, Roman Empire
> Parents: Son of Zebedee and Salome
> Sibling: James
> Death: AD 100
> Ephesus, Asia, Roman Empire"[1]

"St. John the Apostle, also called **Saint John the Evangelist** or **Saint John the Divine.** In Christian tradition, an apostle of Jesus and the author of three letters, the Fourth Gospel, and possibly the Revelation to John in the New Testament. He played a leading role in the early church at Jerusalem.

John was the son of Zebedee, a Galilean fisherman, and Salome. John and his brother St. James were among the first disciples called by Jesus. In The Gospel According to Mark he is always mentioned after James and was no doubt the younger brother. His mother was among those women who ministered to the circle of disciples. James and John were called Boanerges, or "sons of thunder," by Jesus, perhaps because of some character trait such as the zeal exemplified in Mark 9:38 and Luke 9:54, when John and James wanted to call down fire from heaven to punish the Samaritan towns that did not accept Jesus. John and his brother, together with St. Peter, formed an inner nucleus of intimate disciples. In the Fourth Gospel, ascribed by early tradition to John and known formally as The Gospel According to John, the sons of Zebedee are mentioned only once, as being at the shores of the Sea of Tiberias when the risen Lord appeared. Whether the "disciple whom Jesus loved" (who is never named) mentioned in this Gospel is to be identified with John (also not named) is not clear from the text.

John's authoritative position in the church after the Resurrection is shown by his visit with St. Peter to Samaria to lay hands on the new converts there. It is to Peter, James (not the brother of John but "the brother of Jesus"), and John that St. Paul successfully submitted his conversion and mission

---

[1] source: https://en.wikipedia.org/wiki/John_the_Apostle

for recognition. What position John held in the controversy concerning the admission of the Gentiles to the church is not known; the evidence is insufficient for a theory that the Johannine school was anti-Pauline—i.e., opposed to granting Gentiles membership in the church." [2]

"Peter, James, and John were the only witnesses of the raising of Jairus's daughter (Mark 5:35–43). All three also witnessed the transfiguration (Luke 9:28–36), and these same three witnessed the agony in Gethsemane more closely than the other apostles.

John was the disciple who reported to Jesus that they had "forbidden" a nondisciple from casting out demons in Jesus's name (Mark 9:38–41), prompting Jesus to state that "he who is not against us is on our side."

Jesus sent only John and Peter into the city to make the preparation for the final Passover meal, the Last Supper (Luke 22:8–13

Tradition identifies this disciple as Saint John. After the arrest of Jesus, Peter and the "other disciple" (according to Sacred Tradition), John, followed him into the palace of the high priest."[3]

> *"Sacred Tradition or holy Tradition is a theological term used in some Christian traditions, primarily those claiming apostolic succession such as the Catholic, Eastern Orthodox, Oriental Orthodox, Assyrian, and Anglican traditions, to refer to the foundation of the doctrinal and spiritual authority of the Christian.* "[4]

---

[2] **britanica.com, St. John the Apostle, CHRISTIAN APOSTLE**
(WRITTEN BY: Henry Chadwick)
(See Article History)
[3] https://en.wikipedia.org/wiki/John_the_Apostle
[4] CITATION:
The Sacred Tradition information is from the website: www.en.wikipedia.org/wiki/Sacred_tradition

"Alone among the apostles, John remained near Jesus at the foot of the cross on Calvary alongside myrrhbearers and numerous other women."[5]

"Myrrhbearers: are the individuals mentioned in the New Testament who were directly involved in the burial or who discovered the empty tomb following the resurrection of Jesus. The term traditionally refers to the women with myrrh who came to the tomb of Christ early in the morning to find it empty". [6]

"Following the instruction of Jesus from the cross, John took Mary, the mother of Jesus, into his care as the last legacy of Jesus, where John is referred to as the disciple whom Jesus loved (John 19:26–27).

After Jesus's ascension and the descent of the Holy Spirit at Pentecost, John, together with Peter, took a prominent part in the founding and guidance of the Church. He was with Peter at the healing of the lame man at Solomon's Porch in the Temple (Acts 3:1–9), and he was also thrown into prison with Peter (Acts 4:1–13). He went with Peter to visit the newly converted believers in Samaria (Acts 8:14).

According to the Book of Revelation, its author, John the Revelator, was on the island of Patmos "for the word of God and for the testimony of Jesus" when he was honored with the vision contained in Revelation. "[7]

"John 21:24–25 claims that the Gospel of John is based on the written testimony of this disciple."

[5] https://en.wikipedia.org/wiki/John_the_Apostle
[6] en.wikipedia.org › wiki › Myrrhbearers
Myrrhbearers – Wikipedia
[7] https://en.wikipedia.org/wiki/John_the_Apostle
[8] en.wikipedia.org › wiki › Disciple_whom_Jesus_loved

Judas

"Meaning GOD is praised.

> Parents: Cyborea Iscariot, Simon Iscariot (John 6:71; John 12:4; John 13:2, 26)

> Death: Died c. AD 30–33, Jerusalem, Israel" [1]

"Judas Iscariot was, according to the New Testament, one of the twelve original disciples of Jesus Christ, and he was the son of Simon Iscariot. He is known for the kiss and betrayal of Jesus to the Sanhedrin for thirty silver coins.

Though there are varied accounts of his death, the traditional version sees him as having hanged himself following the betrayal, as recorded in Matthew 27:3–5.

His place among the twelve apostles was later filled by Matthias (Acts 1:12–26)."

Despite his notorious role in the Gospel narratives, Judas remains a controversial figure in Christian history. Judas's betrayal, for instance, is seen as setting in motion the events that led to Jesus's crucifixion and resurrection, which according to traditional Christian theology brought salvation to humankind."[2]

"The Gospels of Matthew, Mark, and Luke state that Jesus sent out "the twelve" (including Judas) with power over unclean spirits and with a ministry of preaching and healing: Judas clearly played an active part in this apostolic ministry alongside the other eleven.

> And when he had called unto him his twelve disciples,
> he gave them power against unclean spirits, to cast them

---

[1] Source: https://en.wikipedia.org/wiki/Judas_Iscariot
[2] https://en.wikipedia.org/wiki/Judas_Iscariot

out, and to heal all manner of sickness and all manner of
disease. (Matthew 10:1)

And HE called unto HIM the twelve, and began to send
them forth by two and two; and gave them power over
unclean spirits ... And they cast out many devils, and
anointed with oil many that were sick, and healed them.
(Mark 6:7, 13)

Then HE called his twelve disciples together, and gave
them power and authority over all devils, and to cure
diseases. (Luke 9:1)"[3]

"Matthew directly states that Judas betrayed Jesus for a bribe of "thirty
pieces of silver" by identifying him with a kiss, to arresting soldiers of
the High Priest Caiaphas, who then turned Jesus over to Pontius Pilate's
soldiers (Matthew 26:14–16).

There are several explanations as to why Judas betrayed Jesus. In the earliest
account, in the Gospel of Mark, when he goes to the chief priests to betray
Jesus, he is offered money as a reward, but it is not clear that money is his
motivation (Mark 14:10–11)."[4]

In the Gospel of Matthew account, on the other hand, he asks what they
will pay him for handing Jesus over (Matthew 26:15).

In the Gospel of Luke and the Gospel of John, the devil enters into Judas,
causing him to offer to betray Jesus (John 13:18–30; Luke 22:3).

The Gospel of John account has Judas complaining that money has been
spent on expensive perfumes to anoint Jesus, which could have been spent
on the poor, but adds that he was the keeper of the apostles' purse and used
to steal from it (John 12:5).

---

[3] https://en.wikipedia.org/wiki/Judas_Iscariot
[4] https://en.wikipedia.org/wiki/Judas_Iscariot

There are several explanations as to why Judas betrayed Jesus.

- A possibility is that Judas expected Jesus to overthrow Roman rule of Israel. In this view, Judas is a disillusioned disciple betraying Jesus not so much because he loved money but because he loved his country and thought Jesus had failed it.
- Another possibility is that Jesus was causing unrest likely to increase tensions with the Roman authorities, and they thought He should be restrained until after the Passover, when everyone had gone back home and the commotion had died down.
- Another possibility is that the Gospels suggest Jesus foresaw (John 6:64; Matthew 26:25) and allowed Judas's betrayal (John 13:27–28).
- Another possibility is Jesus allowed the betrayal because it would allow God's plan to be fulfilled.
- Finally, regardless of the betrayal, Jesus was ultimately destined for crucifixion."[5]

---

[5] https://en.wikipedia.org/wiki/Judas_Iscariot

Jude, or Thaddeus

"Birthdate: 1ˢᵗ century AD
Place of Birth: Galilee, Judaea, Roman Empire
Parents: Alphaes Clopas and Mary
Nationality: Roman
Siblings: James the Lesser, Simon the Zealot, Matthew
Death: October 28, 70 AD, Iran" [1]

"Jude the Apostle is generally identified with Thaddeus and is also variously called Jude of James, Jude Thaddaeus, Judas Thaddaeus, or Lebbaeus. His is sometimes identified with Jude, the brother of Jesus, but is clearly distinguished from Judas Iscariot, the apostle who betrayed Jesus prior to His crucifixion

Judas Thaddaeus became known as Jude after early translators of the New Testament from Greek into English sought to distinguish him from Judas Iscariot and subsequently abbreviated his forename.

Most versions of the New Testament in languages other than English and French refer to Judas and Jude by the same name.

Saint Jude's symbol is that of a club. He is also often shown in icons with a flame around his head. This represents his presence at Pentecost, when he received the Holy Spirit with the other apostles. Another symbol of Jude is holding an image of Jesus Christ, in the image of Edessa." [2]

"Image of Edessa

According to Christian tradition, the image of Edessa was a holy relic consisting of a square or rectangle of cloth

---

[1] Source: en.wikipedia.org › wiki › Jude_the_Apostle
Jude the Apostle – Wikipedia
[2] en.wikipedia.org › wiki › Jude_the_Apostle
Jude the Apostle – Wikipedia

upon which a miraculous image of the face of Jesus had been imprinted." [3]

"St. Jude is traditionally depicted carrying the image of Jesus in his hand or close to his chest. This idea comes from a biblical story in which King Abgar of Edessa (a city located in what is now southeast Turkey) asked Jesus to cure him of leprosy and sent an artist to bring him a drawing of Jesus. Impressed with Abgar's great faith, Jesus pressed His face into a cloth and gave it to St. Jude to take to Abgar. Upon seeing Jesus's image, the king was cured, and he converted to Christianity along with most of the people under his rule. This cloth is believed to be the famous Shroud of Jesus, which is currently on display in Turin, Italy." [4]

"After the Last Supper, it was Jude who asked the Lord why he chose to reveal Himself only to the disciples (John 14:22). He received the reply, "If anyone loves me, he will keep my word, and my Father will love him, and we will come to him and make our home with him" (John 14:22f)." [5]

"Tradition holds that Saint Jude preached the Gospel in Judea, Samaria, Idumaea, Syria, Mesopotamia, and Libya." [6]

"In all probability, he spoke both Greek and Aramaic, like almost all of his contemporaries in that area, and he was a farmer by trade. According to the legend, St. Jude was a son of Clopas, and his mother, Mary, was a cousin of the Virgin Mary." [7]

---

[3] en.wikipedia.org › wiki › Jude_the_Apostle
Jude the Apostle – Wikipedia
[4] en.wikipedia.org › wiki › Jude_the_Apostle
Jude the Apostle – Wikipedia
[5] en.wikipedia.org › wiki › Jude_the_Apostle
Jude the Apostle – Wikipedia
[6] en.wikipedia.org › wiki › Jude_the_Apostle
Jude the Apostle – Wikipedia
[7] en.wikipedia.org › wiki › Jude_the_Apostle
Jude the Apostle – Wikipedia

"Tradition has it that Jude's father, Clopas, was martyred because of his forthright and outspoken devotion to the risen Christ."[8]

> "Jude's continued legend has it that St. Jude was born into a Jewish family in Paneas, a town in the Galilee portion of ancient Palestine, the same region that Jesus grew up in. He probably spoke Greek and Aramaic, like many of his contemporaries in that area, and he was a farmer (as many of his family were) by trade.
>
> Jude was described by St. Matthew (13:55) as being one of the "brethren" of Jesus, probably meaning a cousin since the Hebrew word for "brethren" indicates a blood relationship. His mother, Mary, was referred to as a cousin of Jesus' mother Mary, while his father, Cleophas, was the brother of St. Joseph.
>
> Jude had several brothers, no information regarding the names of Jude's other brothers, including St. James, who was another of the original Apostles, Luke 6:16, Acts 1:13. His own first name, "Jude," means giver of joy, while "Thaddeus," another name he was called, means generous and kind.
>
> He was later married, had at least one child, and there are references to his grandchildren living as late as AD 95.
>
> Jude was then called to be one of Jesus 12 Apostles, and began preaching the Good News of Jesus to Jews throughout Galilee, Samaria, and Judea.
>
> St. Jude went to Mesopotamia (present-day Iraq) around AD 37, and became a leader of the Church of The East that St. Thomas established there.

---

[8] en.wikipedia.org › wiki › Jude_the_Apostle
Jude the Apostle – Wikipedia

St. Jude was a true internationalist, traveling throughout Mesopotamia, Libya, Turkey, and Persia with St. Simon, preaching and converting many people to Christianity. He was credited with helping the early creation of the Armenian church, and other places beyond the borders of the Roman Empire.

Around the year AD 60, St. Jude wrote a gospel letter to recent Christian converts in Eastern churches who were under persecution. In it, he warned them against the pseudo-teachers of the day who were spreading false ideas about the early Christian faith. He encouraged them to persevere in the face of the harsh, difficult circumstances they were in, just as their forefathers had done before them. He exhorted them to keep their faith and to stay in the love of God as they had been taught. His inspirational support of these early believers led to him becoming the patron saint of desperate cases.

He is believed to have been martyred in Persia or Syria around 65 AD, together with the apostle Simon the Zealot, with whom he is usually connected. The axe or club that he is often shown holding in pictures symbolizes the way in which he was killed. Truly, he paid the ultimate price for his faith. After his death his body was brought back to Rome and was placed in a crypt beneath St. Peter's Basilica, which people visit to this day.

Now his bones are in the left transept of St. Peter's Basilica under the main altar of St. Joseph in one tomb, with the remains of the apostle Simon the Zealot.

According to another popular tradition, the remains of St. Jude were preserved in an Armenian monastery on an island in the northern part of Issyk-Kul Lake in Kyrgyzstan at least until the mid-fifteenth century. Later legends either deny that the remains are preserved there or claim that they were moved to a yet more desolate stronghold in the Pamir Mountains.

In the Middle Ages, St. Bernard of Clairvaux (France) was a renowned devotee of St. Jude, as was St. Bridget of Sweden who, in a vision, was encouraged by Jesus to turn to St. Jude with faith and confidence. He told her that, in accordance with Jude's surname, Thaddeus (which means generous, courageous, and kind), "he will show himself to be the most willing to give you help. (St. Jude Catholic Church, www.stjudedetroit.org)"[9]

---

[9] Stjudedetroit.org

Matthew or Levi

"The name can mean the following: "Matthew, Greek Gift of God, Levi, Hebrew, joined, attached." [1]

"Birthdate: 1st century
Place of Birth: Palestine
Parents: Alphaeus Clopas, Mary
Siblings: James the Less, Jude, and Simeon the Zealot
Death: AD 51, near Hierapolis or Ethiopia; relics in Salerno, Italy"" [2]

Matthew was also called Levi, which is interpreted a gift hastily given, or a giver of counsel.

Matthew was a gift hastily given by reason of his speedy conversion, and he was a giver of counsel by his salutary preaching. He was great unto God by the perfection of his life and the hand of God by his writing of the gospel. Levi is interpreted as assumed, united, added, or attached; he was assumed from the exaction of the taxes, united to the apostles, added to the number of the evangelists, and attached to the catalogue of the martyrs.

While Matthew the apostle was preaching in Ethiopia, in a city called Nadaber, he found two magicians named Zaroes and Arphaxat, who so were deluded by their sorceries that they lost the use of their limbs and their reason. The magicians were so filled with pride that they made men worship them as gods.

Matthew, having found a hostel in the house of that eunuch of Queen Candace, who was baptized by Philip, unmasked the magicians' tricks in such a way that whatsoever they wrought to the harm of men, he converted to their welfare.

---

[1] (from *The Golden Legend*)
[2] en.wikipedia.org, Matthew the Apostle, Wikipedia

The eunuch asked Matthew how he was able to speak and understand so many tongues. In answer, Matthew explained to him that when the Holy Ghost came upon the apostles, He gave knowledge of all tongues so that, as those who had sought from pride to build a tower reaching to heaven had been stayed therefrom by the confusion of tongues. By the knowledge of tongues, the apostles might build a tower not of stones but of virtues, whereby all who believed might mount to heaven.

Then came one who announced that the magicians were approaching with two dragons, which belched forth a sulfurous fire from their mouths and nostrils and slew all within reach.

The apostle, arming himself with the sign of the cross, went out to them confidently. As soon as the dragons saw him, they fell asleep at his feet. Then said he to the sorcerers, "Where then is your skill! Awaken them if you can: for had I not prayed the Lord, I should have turned upon you the bale, which you thought to inflict upon me!" When the populace gathered together, he commanded the dragons to go away in the name of Jesus, and they went off, harming no one.

Then the apostle preached a wondrous sermon to the people concerning the earthly paradise. He said that it was higher than all mountains and near to heaven; no thorns or brambles grew therein, and the lilies and roses flourished always and waxed never old. There was no old age, with all men remaining ever young. There, the angels made sweet music, and the birds came at one's call. He said that man had been driven out of the earthly paradise, but by the birth of Christ, all were called again to the heavenly paradise.

As he spoke these things to the people, a loud cry of mourning broke out for the king's son, who had died. When the sorcerers were unable to raise him to life, they persuaded the king that his son had been taken up into the company of the gods, and the king should build a temple and make an image in his honor.

But the aforementioned eunuch caused the magicians to be taken prisoners, and he summoned the apostle, who prayed over the youth and restored him to life. At this, the king, whose name was Egippus, sent heralds throughout his realm, proclaiming, "Come and see God hiding in the form of a man!" They came therefore with golden crowns and divers kinds of victims, wishing to sacrifice to him. But Matthew forbade them, saying, "Men, what do ye? I am not a god, but the servant of Jesus Christ!" At his command, they then used their offerings of gold and silver to build a great church, which they erected within thirty days. In this church, the apostle presided for three and thirty years and converted all of Egypt to the faith. King Egippus was baptized with his wife and all the people. The apostle also dedicated the king's daughter, Ephigenia, to God and set her over more than two hundred virgins.

Sometime later, Hirtacus succeeded the king and, lusting after the virgin Ephigenia, promised the apostle the half of his kingdom if he would prevail upon her to become his wife. The apostle answered that following the usage of his predecessor, he should come to the church on the following Sunday and, in the presence of Ephigenia and the other virgins, hear how good was godly matrimony.

Thither the king hastened with joy, thinking that the apostle meant to urge Ephigenia to marry. Matthew therefore preached for a long time to the virgins and the assembled populace concerning the good of matrimony; wherefore he was much praised by the king, Then, commanding silence, the apostle continued.

> Because marriage is a good thing, we who are present well know that if a servant dared to molest the king's spouse, he would deserve not only the king's displeasure, but death besides; and this not because he wished to take a wife, but because he violated the king's marriage by carrying off his wife. And thou, O king, who knowest that Ephigenia is espoused to the eternal King, how canst thou purloin the spouse of One mightier than thou, and take her to wife?

When he heard these words, the king was consumed with rage and went out of the church. The apostle, intrepid and unmoved, exhorted all to patience and constancy, and he blessed Ephigenia and the other virgins, who had prostrated themselves at his feet. After the mass, the king sent a swordsman, who came behind Matthew as he stood at the altar with his hands raised to heaven in prayer, drove his sword into his back, and so consummated the apostle's martyrdom.

When the populace heard these tidings, they ran to the king's palace to set it afire, but they were restrained by the priests and deacons and made gladsome celebration for the saint's martyrdom. Meanwhile, the king could not bend Ephigenia to his will, either by matrons whom he dispatched to her or by the artifices of the magicians. He therefore heaped up a great fire about her house in order to destroy her and the other virgins. But the apostle appeared to them and warded the flames from the house, and it swept to the royal palace and burned it to the ground, with the king and his only son barely escaping. Thereupon the king's son was seized by the devil and sped to the apostle's tomb, loudly proclaiming his father's sins, while the infamous father was stricken with an incurable leprosy and killed himself with his own sword.

The people then chose Ephigenia's brother, who had been baptized by the apostle, to be their king. He reigned for seventy years and then gave his throne to his son. He enhanced the Christian worship lavishly and filled the whole province of Egypt with the churches of Christ. As for Zaroes and Arphaxat, they fled to Persia the very day that Matthew raised the king's son to life, but there Simon and Jude vanquished them.

We may note that in Saint Matthew, four things are worthy of consideration. The first is his swiftness to obey. As soon as Christ called him, he quit his customhouse, leaving his tax accounts incomplete without fear of his masters, and devoted himself completely to Christ. This ready obedience has been a source of error to some, as Jerome recounts in his commentary on that place of the gospel.

> Porphyry and the Emperor Julian find proof therein either
> of the ignorance of a lying chronicler, or of the witlessness of
> them that so promptly followed the Saviour, as if they went
> off after the first man who called them, without any reason

whatsoever. But there is no doubt that the apostles, before they believed in Him, had seen the many signs of His power, which went before Him. And of a surety, the very splendour and majesty of His hidden godhead, which shone even in His human countenance, were enough to draw them the first time they looked upon him. For if a magnet has power to attract rings and bits of iron, how much the more can the Lord of all creation draw to Himself those whom He will!

The second virtue is his bounty or generosity, whereby he made Him a great feast in his house. The feast was great not so much because of the sumptuous arrangements as for the following reasons. first, Matthew's will and intention, for he received the Lord with great love and desire; second, the mystery involved, which is explained in the *Gloss* on Saint Luke ("He who receives Christ into his inward abode, is filled with the sweetness of abounding delights"); third, Christ's teachings on that occasion, such as "I will have mercy and not Sacrifice" and "They that are whole need not the physician, but they that are sick"; fourth, the guests who were invited, namely Christ and His disciples.

The third virtue is his humility, which is manifested in a twofold way. First, Matthew himself avows that he was a publican. The other evangelists, as the *Gloss* says, did not put down the common name because of the reverence and honor due to an evangelist. Because the just man is the first to accuse himself, he calls himself Matthew and a publican in order to show that no one who is converted should mistrust his salvation, when a publican could suddenly become an apostle and an evangelist. Second, he bore injuries patiently.

When the Pharisees murmured because Christ went down to a sinful man, he could rightly have answered them, "You rather are miserable and sinful men, who, deeming yourselves just, flee the physician; whereas I can no longer be called a sinner, who take refuge with the physician of salvation, and hide not my wounds from Him!"

Last, we may note the great honor in which his gospel is held in the Church, for it is read more often than the other gospels, just as the Psalms of David and the Epistles of Saint Paul are recited more frequently than the other sacred writings.

The reason for this is as follows. Saint James says that there are three kinds of sin: pride, lust, and avarice. Saul, who had his name from the proud King Saul, committed the sin of pride when he persecuted the Church of God beyond measure.

David committed the sin of lust when he not only fell into adultery but also, on account of his adultery, took the life of his most faithful soldier, Urias.

Matthew committed the sin of avarice by his panting Lyreed (Lyreed is a word that was an error. It should be greed, or ill-gotten gain) for filthy lucre; for he was a keeper of the customs. The customhouse, or teloneum, as Isidore says, is a place at a seaport where ships and seamen pay tolls on their goods. The tolls, according to Bede, are called *telos* in Greek and *vectigal* in Latin. These three men were therefore sinners. Yet their repentance was so pleasing to the Lord that not only did He forgive them, but He also heaped His gifts upon them in greater abundance.

Of the most cruel persecutor, He made a faithful preacher. Of the adulterer and murderer, He made a prophet and a psalmist. Of the miser and money seeker, He made an apostle and an evangelist. Therefore the words of these three are read to us more frequently so that none who wishes to be converted may despair of pardon, when grace wrought such wonders in such great sinners.

The gospel that Matthew wrote with his own hand was covered with the bones of Saint Barnabas, in the Year of the Lord 500. Saint Barnabas ever carried this gospel with him and placed it upon the heads of the sick; all were cured by the faith of Barnabas and by the merits of Matthew.

http://projects.mcah.columbia.edu/medieval-architecture/htm/sw/ma_ sw_gloss_matthew.htm

Source: Saint Matthew the Apostle

(September 211)

Peter, or Simon Peter

"Birth Name: Shimon, (Simeon, Simon)
Birthdate: c. 4 BC
Place of Birth: Bethsaida, Gaulanitis, Syria, Roman Empire
Parents: John (or Jonah or Jona)
Occupation: Fisherman, clergyman
Death: between AD 64 and 68" [1]

"Peter's original name, as indicated in the New Testament, was "Simon" or Simeon (only in Acts 15:14 and 2 Peter 1:1 The Simon/Simeon variation has been explained as reflecting "the well-known custom among Jews at the time of giving the name of a famous patriarch or personage of the Old Testament to a male child along with a similar sounding Greek/Roman name" [1]

"Peter's life story is told in the four gospels, the Acts of the Apostles, New Testament letters, the noncanonical Gospel of the Hebrews, and other early Church accounts of his life and death. Peter became the first listed apostle ordained by Jesus in the early Church." [2]

"Peter was a fisherman in Bethsaida. The three Synoptic Gospels recount how Peter's mother-in-law was healed by Jesus at their home in Capernaum; this passage clearly depicts Peter as being married (Mark 1:30), and 1 Corinthians 9:5 states Cephas (John 1:42), who is Peter, and his wife traveled with him on his journeys. [3]

In the Synoptic Gospels, Peter (then Simon) was a fisherman along with his brother Andrew and the sons of Zebedee, James and John. The Gospel of John also depicts Peter fishing, even after the resurrection of Jesus, in the

---

[1] Source: www.en.wikipedia.org, St. Peter Wikipedia
[2] : www.en.wikipedia.org, St. Peter Wikipedia
[3] : www.en.wikipedia.org, St. Peter Wikipedia

story "The Catch of 153 Fish." In Matthew and Mark, Jesus called Simon and his brother Andrew "fishers of men." [4]

"Synoptic Gospels

The gospels of Matthew, Mark, and Luke are referred to as the Synoptic Gospels because they include many of the same stories, often in a similar sequence and in similar wording. They stand in contrast to John, whose content is comparatively distinct. The term *synoptic* (Latin: synopticus; Greek: translit. synoptikós) comes via Latin from the synopsis—that is, "(a) seeing all together, synopsis." The sense of the word in English, the one specifically applied to these three gospels, of "giving an account of the events from the same point of view or under the same general aspect" is a modern one." [5]

"A Franciscan church is built upon the traditional site of Apostle Peter's house. In Luke, Simon Peter owns the boat that Jesus uses to preach to the multitudes who were pressing on him at the shore of Lake Gennesaret. Jesus then amazes Simon and his companions James and John (Andrew is not mentioned) by telling them to lower their nets, whereupon they catch a huge number of fish." [6]

"In a dialogue between Jesus and His disciples (Matthew 16:13–19), Jesus asks, "Who do people say that the Son of Man is?" The disciples give various answers. When he asks, "Who do *you* say that I am?" Simon Peter answers, "You are the Messiah, the Son of the living God." Jesus then declares,

> Blessed are you, Simon son of Jonah, for this was not revealed to you by flesh and blood, but by my Father in heaven. And I tell you that you are Peter (Petros), and on this rock (petra) I will build my church, and the gates of Hades will not overcome it. I will give you the keys of the

---

[4] : www.en.wikipedia.org, St. Peter Wikipedia
[5] : www.en.wikipedia.org, St. Peter Wikipedia
[6] : www.en.wikipedia.org, St. Peter Wikipedia

kingdom of heaven; whatever you bind on earth will be bound in heaven, and whatever you loose on earth will be loosed in heaven." [7]

"All four gospels recount that during the Last Supper, Jesus foretold that Peter would deny him three times before the following cockcrow ("before the cock crows twice" in Mark's account)."[8]

"The three Synoptic Gospels (Matthew, Mark, and Luke) as well as John describe the three denials as follows.

1. A denial when a female servant of the high priest spots Simon Peter, saying that he had been with Jesus. According to Mark (but not in all manuscripts), "the rooster crowed." Only Luke and John mention a fire by which Peter was warming himself among other people. According to Luke, Peter was "sitting"; according to John, he was "standing."
2. A denial when Simon Peter had gone out to the gateway, away from the firelight, but the same servant girl (Mark) or another servant girl (Matthew) or a man (Luke and also John, for whom, though, this is the third denial) told the bystanders he was a follower of Jesus. According to John, "the rooster crowed."
3. A denial came when Peter's Galilean accent was taken as proof that he was indeed a disciple of Jesus. According to Matthew, Mark, and Luke, "the rooster crowed." John, though, does not mention the Galilean accent." [9]

"In the Gospel of Luke is a record of Christ telling Peter, "Simon, Simon, behold, Satan hath desired to have you, that he may sift you as wheat: but I have prayed for thee, that thy faith fail not: and when thou art converted, strengthen thy brethren." In a reminiscent scene in John's epilogue, Peter affirms three times that he loves Jesus." [10]

---

[7] : www.en.wikipedia.org, St. Peter Wikipedia
[8] : www.en.wikipedia.org, St. Peter Wikipedia
[9] : www.en.wikipedia.org, St. Peter Wikipedia
[10] : www.en.wikipedia.org, St. Peter Wikipedia

"According to Christian tradition, Peter was crucified in Rome under Emperor Nero Caesar Augustus. It is traditionally held that he was crucified upside down at his own request, since he saw himself unworthy to be crucified in the same way as Jesus. Tradition holds that he was crucified at the site of the Clementine Chapel. His remains are said to be those contained in the underground Confessio of Peter's Basilica, where Pope Paul VI announced in 1968 the excavated discovery of a first-century Roman cemetery." [11]

---

[11] : www.en.wikipedia.org, St. Peter Wikipedia

Philip

> "Birthdate: AD 5
> Place of Birth: Bethsaida
> Death: AD 80, Hierapolis, Turkey
> Buried: Santi Apostoli, Rome, Italy" [1]

"Philip the Apostle (Greek: *Philippos*) was one of the twelve apostles of Jesus. Later Christian traditions describe Philip as the apostle who preached in Greece, Syria, and Phrygia." [1]

"The Synoptic Gospels list Philip as one of the apostles. The Gospel of John recounts Philip's calling as a disciple of Jesus. Philip is described as a disciple from the city of Bethsaida, and the evangelist John connects him with Andrew and Peter, who were from the same town. He also was among those surrounding John the Baptist when the latter first pointed out Jesus as the Lamb of God. It was Philip who first introduced Nathanael (sometimes identified with Bartholomew) to Jesus. According to Butler, Philip was among those attending the wedding at Cana." [2]

"Of the four Gospels, Philip figures most prominently in the Gospel of John. Later, he appears as a link to the Greek community. Philip bore a Greek name, may have spoken Greek, and may have been known to the Greek pilgrims in Jerusalem. He advises Andrew that certain Greeks wish to meet Jesus, and together they inform Jesus of this (John 12:21). During the Last Supper, when Philip asked Jesus to show them the Father, he provides Jesus the opportunity to teach his disciples about the unity of the Father and the Son." [3]

"Philip the Apostle should not be confused with Philip the Evangelist, who was appointed with Stephen to oversee charitable distributions (Acts 6:5)." [4]

---

[1] Source: en.wikipedia.org, Philip, The Apostle Wikipedia
[2] Philip, The Apostle Wikipedia
[3] Philip, The Apostle Wikipedia
[4] Philip, The Apostle Wikipedia

"The interesting thing about Philip, one of the twelve, is that he was personally reached by Jesus Himself. Whereas Philip brought Nathanael to Jesus, and Andrew brought Peter to Jesus, no one brought Philip to Jesus. Instead, Jesus came right to him. John's Gospel tells us, "The following day Jesus wanted to go to Galilee, and He found Philip and said to him, 'Follow Me'" (John 1:43). Normally God reaches people through people, but this was an exception to the rule." [5]

"Philip is asked by Jesus how to feed five thousand people, when Jesus was about to perform a miracle and feed a multitude of people with a small amount of food. Jesus asked Philip where they should buy the bread to feed the people. But Jesus was testing Philip, because Jesus already knew that He would perform a miracle (John 6:5–6)" [6]

"After the resurrection of Jesus, Philip was sent with his sister, Marianne, and Bartholomew to preach in Greece, Phrygia, and Syria. Included in the Acts of Philip is an appendix, entitled "Of the Journey of Philip the Apostle: From the Fifteenth Act Until the End, and Among Them the Martyrdom." This appendix gives an account of Philip's martyrdom in the city of Hierapolis. According to this account, through a miraculous healing and his preaching, Philip converted the wife of the proconsul of the city." [7]

"This enraged the proconsul, and he had Philip, Bartholomew, and Marianne tortured. Philip and Bartholomew were then crucified upside down, and Philip preached from his cross. As a result of Philip's preaching, the crowd released Bartholomew from his cross, but Philip insisted that they not release him, and Philip died on the cross." [8]

---

[5] Philip, The Apostle Wikipedia
[6] Philip, The Apostle Wikipedia
[7] Philip, The Apostle Wikipedia
[8] Philip, The Apostle Wikipedia

Simon the Canaanite, Zealot

> "Place of Birth: Judea
> Parents: Alphaeus Clopas, Mary
> Siblings: James the Less, Jude, Matthew
> Death: c. AD 65 or c. AD 107
> Place of Death: Disputed; possibly Pelia, Armenia, Suanir, Persia, Edessa, or Caistor" [1]

"Simon the Zealot, Simon Kananaios, or Simon Cananeus was one of the most obscure among the apostles of Jesus." [2]

"The name Simon occurs in all of the Synoptic Gospels." [3]

"In the Gospels of Mark and Matthew, he bears the epithet *Kananaios*, or the Cananaean, often wrongly interpreted to mean "from Cana" or "from Canaan." *Kananaios* is the Greek transliteration of an Aramaic word *qan⬚ anaya*, meaning "the Zealot," the title given him by Luke in his gospel and in Acts. It is uncertain whether he was one of the group of Zealots, the Jewish nationalistic party before AD 70." [4]

"To distinguish him from Simon Peter, he is called Kananaios, Canaanite, (Matthew 10:4) or Kananites (Mark 3:18), and in the list of apostles in Luke 6:15, repeated in Acts 1:13, he is Zelotes, the "Zealot." Both titles derive from the Hebrew word *qana*, meaning zealous." [5]

"Nothing further is known about him from the New Testament. He supposedly preached the Gospel in Egypt and then joined the apostle St.

---

[1] Source: wikipedia.com, Simon the Zealot, Wikipedia

[2] Simon the Zealot, Wikipedia

[3] **Simon the Zealot, Wikipedia**

[4] britannica.com, Saint Simon the Apostle, **CHRISTIAN APOSTLE**
(WRITTEN BY: The Editors of Encyclopaedia Britannica)
(See Article History)

[5] **britannica.com, Saint Simon the Apostle, CHRISTIAN APOSTLE**
(WRITTEN BY: The Editors of Encyclopaedia Britannica)
(See Article History 5)

Judas (Thaddaeus) in Persia, where, according to the apocryphal Acts of Simon and Judas, he was martyred by being cut in half with a saw, one of his chief iconographic symbols (another being a book). According to St. Basil the Great, the fourth-century Cappadocian father, Simon died peacefully at Edessa." [6]

[6] **britannica.com, Saint Simon the Apostle**, **CHRISTIAN APOSTLE**
(WRITTEN BY: The Editors of Encyclopaedia Britannica)
(See Article History 6)

Thomas Doubting, Didymus

"Name Means: Twin" [1]
"Place of Birth: Galilee, Israel
Occupation: Fisherman
Death: December 21, 72 AD, Mylapore, India" [2]

"Thomas the Apostle (*Thoma Sheliha*), also called Didymus ("twin"), was one of the Twelve Apostles of Jesus according to the New Testament. Thomas is commonly known as "Doubting Thomas' because he doubted Jesus' resurrection when first told of it (as related in the Gospel of John alone); later, he confessed his faith, "My Lord and my God," on seeing Jesus' crucifixion wounds." [3]

"Traditionally, Thomas is believed to have travelled outside the Roman Empire to preach the Gospel, travelling as far as Tamilakam which are the states of Kerala and Tamil Nadu in present-day India. "[4]

"According to tradition, Thomas reached Muziris, (modern-day North Paravur and Kodungalloor in the state of Kerala, India) in AD 52 and converted several people, founding what today are known as Saint Thomas Christians or Mar Thoma Nazranis " [5]

---

[1] Source: britanica.com, St. Thomas, **CHRISTIAN APOSTLE** (WRITTEN BY: The Editors of Encyclopaedia Britannica) (LAST UPDATED: Jan 1, 2020 See Article History)
[2] en, wikipedia.org, Thomas the Apostle, Wikipedia
[3] britanica.com, St. Thomas, **CHRISTIAN APOSTLE** (WRITTEN BY: The Editors of Encyclopaedia Britannica) (LAST UPDATED: Jan 1, 2020 See Article History)
[4] **britanica.com, St. Thomas, CHRISTIAN APOSTLE** (WRITTEN BY: The Editors of Encyclopaedia Britannica) (LAST UPDATED: Jan 1, 2020 See Article History)
[5] **britanica.com, St. Thomas, CHRISTIAN APOSTLE** (WRITTEN BY: The Editors of Encyclopaedia Britannica) (LAST UPDATED: Jan 1, 2020 See Article History)

"After his death, the reputed relics of Saint Thomas the Apostle were enshrined as far as Mesopotamia in the 3rd century, and later moved to various places." [6]

"In 1258, some of the relics were brought to Ortona, in Abruzzo, Italy, where they have been held in the Church of Saint Thomas the Apostle." [7]

"He is often regarded as the patron saint of India, and the name *Thoma* remains quite popular among Saint Thomas Christians of India." [8]

"Thomas first speaks in the Gospel of John. In John 11:16, when Lazarus had recently died, the apostles do not wish to go back to Judea, where some Jews had attempted to stone Jesus. Thomas says: "Let us also go, that we may die with him. (KJV)" [9]

"Thomas speaks again in John 14:5. There, Jesus had just explained that he was going away to prepare a heavenly home for his followers, and that one day they would join him there. Thomas reacted by saying, "Lord, we know not whither thou goest; and how can we know the way?" John 20:24–29 tells how doubting Thomas was skeptical at first when he heard that Jesus had risen from the dead

[6] **britanica.com, St. Thomas, CHRISTIAN APOSTLE**
(WRITTEN BY: The Editors of Encyclopaedia Britannica)
(LAST UPDATED: Jan 1, 2020 See Article History)
[7] **britanica.com, St. Thomas CHRISTIAN APOSTLE**
(WRITTEN BY: The Editors of Encyclopaedia Britannica)
(LAST UPDATED: Jan 1, 2020 See Article History)
[8] **britanica.com, St. Thomas, CHRISTIAN APOSTLE**
WRITTEN BY: The Editors of Encyclopaedia Britannica
LAST UPDATED: Jan 1, 2020 See Article History
[9] **britanica.com, St. Thomas, CHRISTIAN APOSTLE**
(WRITTEN BY: The Editors of Encyclopaedia Britannica)
(LAST UPDATED: Jan 1, 2020 See Article History)

and appeared to the other apostles, saying, "Except I shall see on his hands the print of the nails, and put my finger into the print of the nails, and thrust my hand into his side, I will not believe." "[10]

"But when Jesus appeared later and invited Thomas to touch his wounds and behold him, Thomas showed his belief by saying, "My Lord and my God." Jesus then said, "Thomas, because thou hast seen me, thou hast believed: blessed are they that have not seen, and yet have believed." "[11]

"Thomas is traditionally believed to have sailed to India in AD 52 (but there is evidence of his being in Taxila in AD 43, where he did not have success) to spread the Christian faith, and is believed to have landed at the port of Muziris, (modern-day North Paravur and Kodungalloor in modern-day Kerala state) where there was a Jewish community at the time. The port was destroyed in 1341 by a massive flood that realigned the coasts. He is believed by the Saint Thomas Christian tradition to have established seven churches (communities) in Kerala. These churches are at Kodungallur, Palayoor, Kottakkavu, (Paravur) Kikkamangalam, Niranam, Nilackal (Chayal), Kollam and Thiruvithamcode (half church)." [12]

"Thomas baptized several families, namely Pakalomattom, Sankarapuri, Thayyil, Payyappilly, Kalli, Kaliyankal,

---

[10] **britanica.com, St. Thomas CHRISTIAN APOSTLE**
(WRITTEN BY: The Editors of Encyclopaedia Britannica)
(LAST UPDATED: Jan 1, 2020 See Article History)
[11] **britanica.com, St. Thomas, CHRISTIAN APOSTLE**
(WRITTEN BY: The Editors of Encyclopaedia Britannica)
(LAST UPDATED: Jan 1, 2020 See Article History)
[12] **britanica.com, St. Thomas, CHRISTIAN APOSTLE**
(WRITTEN BY: The Editors of Encyclopaedia Britannica)
(LAST UPDATED: Jan 1, 2020 See Article History)

Pattamukku. Other families claim to have origins almost as far back as these, and the religious historian Robert Eric Frykenberg notes that "Whatever dubious historicity may be attached to such local traditions, there can be little doubt as to their great antiquity or to their great appeal in popular imagination." "[13]

"It was to a land of dark people he was sent, to clothe them by Baptism in white robes. His grateful dawn dispelled India's painful darkness. It was his mission to espouse India to the One-Begotten. The merchant is blessed for having so great a treasure. Edessa thus became the blessed city by possessing the greatest pearl India could yield. Thomas works miracles in India, and at Edessa Thomas is destined to baptize peoples perverse and steeped in darkness, and that in the land of India." [14]

"According to Syrian Christian tradition, Saint Thomas was allegedly martyred at St. Thomas Mount, in Chennai, in AD 72, July 3rd, and his body was interred in Mylapore. Ephrem the Syrian states that the Apostle was martyred in India, and that his relics were taken then to Edessa. This is the earliest known record of his martyrdom." [15]

As the disciples were, we as disciples of Jesus should be today. The following are scriptures on the supernatural power and authority given to the disciples before Jesus's ascension.

[13] **britanica.com, St. Thomas, CHRISTIAN APOSTLE** (WRITTEN BY: The Editors of Encyclopaedia Britannica) (LAST UPDATED: Jan 1, 2020 See Article History 13)
[14] **britanica.com, St. Thomas, CHRISTIAN APOSTLE** (WRITTEN BY: The Editors of Encyclopaedia Britannica) (LAST UPDATED: Jan 1, 2020 See Article History)
[15] britanica.com, **St. Thomas, CHRISTIAN APOSTLE** (WRITTEN BY: The Editors of Encyclopaedia Britannica) (LAST UPDATED: Jan 1, 2020 See Article History)

And when he had called unto him his twelve disciples, he gave them power against unclean spirits, to cast them out, and to heal all manner of sickness and all manner of disease. (Matthew 10:1)

And he ordained twelve, that they should be with him, and that he might send them forth to preach, And to have power to heal sicknesses, and to cast out devils. (Mark 3:14–15)

And he called unto him the twelve, and began to send them forth by two and two; and gave them power over unclean spirits. (Mark 6:7)

Then he called his twelve disciples together, and gave them power and authority over all devils, and to cure diseases. (Luke 9:1)

Moreover, these are the scriptures on the supernatural acts of the twelve disciples after Jesus's ascension.

Now Peter and John went up together into the temple at the hour of prayer, being the ninth hour.

And a certain man lame from his mother's womb was carried, whom they laid daily at the gate of the temple which is called Beautiful, to ask alms of them that entered into the temple;

Who seeing Peter and John about to go into the temple asked an alms.

And Peter, fastening his eyes upon him with John, said, Look on us.

And he gave heed unto them, expecting to receive something of them.

Then Peter said, Silver and gold have I none; but such as I have give I thee: In the name of Jesus Christ of Nazareth rise up and walk.

And he took him by the right hand, and lifted him up: and immediately his feet and anklebones received strength.

And he leaping up stood, and walked, and entered with them into the temple, walking, and leaping, and praising God.

And all the people saw him walking and praising God:

And they knew that it was he which sat for alms at the Beautiful gate of the temple: and they were filled with wonder and amazement at that which had happened unto him. (Acts 3:1–10)

Now when they saw the boldness of Peter and John, and perceived that they were unlearned and ignorant men, they marvelled; and they took knowledge of them, that they had been with Jesus.

And beholding the man which was healed standing with them, they could say nothing against it.

But when they had commanded them to go aside out of the council, they conferred among themselves,

Saying, What shall we do to these men? for that indeed a notable miracle hath been done by them is manifest to all them that dwell in Jerusalem; and we cannot deny it. (Acts 4:13–16)

And by the hands of the apostles were many signs and wonders wrought among the people; (and they were all with one accord in Solomon's porch. (Acts 5:12)

Insomuch that they brought forth the sick into the streets, and laid them on beds and couches, that at the least the shadow of Peter passing by might overshadow some of them.

There came also a multitude out of the cities round about unto Jerusalem, bringing sick folks, and them which were vexed with unclean spirits: and they were healed every one. (Acts 5:15–16)

Supernatural Acts of Peter

"So that they brought the sick out into the streets and laid them on beds and couches, that at least the shadow of Peter passing by might fall on some of them" (Acts 5:15).

Aeneas is healed: "And there he found a certain man named Aeneas, which had kept his bed eight years, and was sick of the palsy. And Peter said unto him, Aeneas, Jesus Christ makes thee whole: arise, and make thy bed. And he arose immediately. And all that dwelt at Lydda and Saron saw him, and turned to the Lord" (Acts 9:33–34).

Tabitha (Dorcas) is raised from the dead by Peter: "And it came to pass in those days, that she was sick, and died: whom when they had washed, they laid her in an upper chamber ... But Peter put them all forth [Mark 5:40], and kneeled down, and prayed; and turning him to the body said, Tabitha, arise. And she opened her eyes: and when she saw Peter, she sat up. And he gave her his hand, and lifted her up, and when he had called the saints and widows, presented her alive" (Acts 9:36–41).

Ananias and Sapphira are punished: "Then Peter said unto her, How is it that ye have agreed together to tempt the Spirit of the Lord? behold, the feet of them which have buried thy husband are at the door, and shall carry thee out" (Acts 5:1–10).

Supernatural Acts by Philip

"And the people with one accord gave heed unto those things which Philip spake, hearing and seeing the miracles which he did. For unclean spirits, crying with a loud voice, came out of many who were possessed; and many who were paralyzed and lame were healed" (Acts 8:6–7).

Philip transported by the Spirit of the Lord out of the desert to Azotus: "And when they were come up out of the water, the Spirit of the Lord caught away Philip, that the eunuch saw him no more: and he went on his way rejoicing But Philip was found at Azotus" (Acts 8:26–40).

CHAPTER 3

After Jesus chose His twelve disciples, He continued to perform many miracles, wonders, and teachings with the disciples before the Last Supper. These teachings were as follows.

The Beatitudes: Jesus's Sermon on the Mount

> And Jesus went about all Galilee, teaching in their synagogues, and preaching the gospel of the kingdom, and healing all manner of sickness and all manner of disease among the people.
>
> And his fame went throughout all Syria: and they brought unto him all sick people that were taken with divers diseases and torments, and those which were possessed with devils, and those which were lunatick, and those that had the palsy; and he healed them.
>
> And there followed him great multitudes of people from Galilee, and from Decapolis, and from Jerusalem, and from Judaea, and from beyond Jordan.
>
> And seeing the multitudes, he went up into a mountain: and when he was set, his disciples came unto him:
>
> And he opened his mouth, and taught them, saying,

Blessed are the poor in spirit: for theirs is the kingdom of heaven.

Blessed are they that mourn: for they shall be comforted.

Blessed are the meek: for they shall inherit the earth.

Blessed are they which do hunger and thirst after righteousness: for they shall be filled.

Blessed are the merciful: for they shall obtain mercy.

Blessed are the pure in heart: for they shall see God.

Blessed are the peacemakers: for they shall be called the children of God.

Blessed are they which are persecuted for righteousness' sake: for theirs is the kingdom of heaven.

Blessed are ye, when men shall revile you, and persecute you, and shall say all manner of evil against you falsely, for my sake.

Rejoice, and be exceeding glad: for great is your reward in heaven: for so persecuted they the prophets which were before you. (Matthew 4:23–5:12)

Salt and Light

Ye are the salt of the earth: but if the salt have lost his savour, wherewith shall it be salted? it is thenceforth good for nothing, but to be cast out, and to be trodden under foot of men.

Ye are the light of the world. A city that is set on an hill cannot be hid.

Neither do men light a candle, and put it under a bushel, but on a candlestick; and it giveth light unto all that are in the house.

Let your light so shine before men, that they may see your good works, and glorify your Father which is in heaven. (Matthew 5:13–16)

Christ Came to Fulfill the Law

Think not that I am come to destroy the law, or the prophets: I am not come to destroy, but to fulfil.

For verily I say unto you, Till heaven and earth pass, one jot or one tittle shall in no wise pass from the law, till all be fulfilled.

Whosoever therefore shall break one of these least commandments, and shall teach men so, he shall be called the least in the kingdom of heaven: but whosoever shall do and teach them, the same shall be called great in the kingdom of heaven.

For I say unto you, That except your righteousness shall exceed the righteousness of the scribes and Pharisees, ye shall in no case enter into the kingdom of heaven. (Matthew 5:17–20)

Anger

Ye have heard that it was said of them of old time, Thou shalt not kill; and whosoever shall kill shall be in danger of the judgment:

But I say unto you, That whosoever is angry with his brother without a cause shall be in danger of the judgment: and whosoever shall say to his brother, Raca, shall be in danger of the council: but whosoever shall say, Thou fool, shall be in danger of hell fire.

Therefore if thou bring thy gift to the altar, and there rememberest that thy brother hath ought against thee;

Leave there thy gift before the altar, and go thy way; first be reconciled to thy brother, and then come and offer thy gift. (Matthew 5: 212–24)

Lust

Ye have heard that it was said by them of old time, Thou shalt not commit adultery:

But I say unto you, That whosoever looketh on a woman to lust after her hath committed adultery with her already in his heart.

And if thy right eye offend thee, pluck it out, and cast it from thee: for it is profitable for thee that one of thy members should perish, and not that thy whole body should be cast into hell.

And if thy right hand offend thee, cut it off, and cast it from thee: for it is profitable for thee that one of thy members should perish, and not that thy whole body should be cast into hell. (Matthew 5:27–30)

Divorce

It hath been said, Whosoever shall put away his wife, let him give her a writing of divorcement:

But I say unto you, That whosoever shall put away his wife, saving for the cause of fornication, causeth her to commit adultery: and whosoever shall marry her that is divorced committeth adultery. (Matthew 5:31–32)

Oaths

Again, ye have heard that it hath been said by them of old time, Thou shalt not forswear thyself, but shalt perform unto the Lord thine oaths:

But I say unto you, Swear not at all; neither by heaven; for it is God's throne:

Nor by the earth; for it is his footstool: neither by Jerusalem; for it is the city of the great King.

Neither shalt thou swear by thy head, because thou canst not make one hair white or black.

But let your communication be, Yea, yea; Nay, nay: for whatsoever is more than these cometh of evil. (Matthew 5: 33–37)

Retaliation

Ye have heard that it hath been said, An eye for an eye, and a tooth for a tooth:

But I say unto you, That ye resist not evil: but whosoever shall smite thee on thy right cheek, turn to him the other also.

And if any man will sue thee at the law, and take away thy coat, let him have thy cloak also.

And whosoever shall compel thee to go a mile, go with him twain.

Give to him that asketh thee, and from him that would borrow of thee turn not thou away. (Matthew 5:38–42)

Love Your Enemies

Ye have heard that it hath been said, Thou shalt love thy neighbour, and hate thine enemy.

But I say unto you, Love your enemies, bless them that curse you, do good to them that hate you, and pray for them which despitefully use you, and persecute you;

That ye may be the children of your Father which is in heaven: for he maketh his sun to rise on the evil and on the good, and sendeth rain on the just and on the unjust.

For if ye love them which love you, what reward have ye? do not even the publicans the same?

And if ye salute your brethren only, what do ye more than others? do not even the publicans so?

Be ye therefore perfect, even as your Father which is in heaven is perfect. (Matthew 5:43–48)

Giving to the Needy

Take heed that ye do not your alms before men, to be seen of them: otherwise ye have no reward of your Father which is in heaven.

Therefore when thou doest thine alms, do not sound a trumpet before thee, as the hypocrites do in the synagogues and in the streets, that they may have glory of men. Verily I say unto you, They have their reward.

But when thou doest alms, let not thy left hand know what thy right hand doeth:

That thine alms may be in secret: and thy Father which seeth in secret himself shall reward thee openly. (Matthew 6:1–4)

The Lord's Prayer

And when thou prayest, thou shalt not be as the hypocrites are: for they love to pray standing in the synagogues and in the corners of the streets, that they may be seen of men. Verily I say unto you, They have their reward.

But thou, when thou prayest, enter into thy closet, and when thou hast shut thy door, pray to thy Father which is in secret; and thy Father which seeth in secret shall reward thee openly.

But when ye pray, use not vain repetitions, as the heathen do: for they think that they shall be heard for their much speaking.

Be not ye therefore like unto them: for your Father knoweth what things ye have need of, before ye ask him.

After this manner therefore pray ye: Our Father which art in heaven, Hallowed be thy name.

Thy kingdom come, Thy will be done in earth, as it is in heaven.

Give us this day our daily bread.

And forgive us our debts, as we forgive our debtors.

And lead us not into temptation, but deliver us from evil: For thine is the kingdom, and the power, and the glory, for ever. Amen.

For if ye forgive men their trespasses, your heavenly Father will also forgive you:

But if ye forgive not men their trespasses, neither will your Father forgive your trespasses. (Matthew 6:5–15)

Fasting

Moreover when ye fast, be not, as the hypocrites, of a sad countenance: for they disfigure their faces, that they may appear unto men to fast. Verily I say unto you, They have their reward.

But thou, when thou fastest, anoint thine head, and wash thy face;

That thou appear not unto men to fast, but unto thy Father which is in secret: and thy Father, which seeth in secret, shall reward thee openly. (Matthew 6:16–18)

Lay Up Treasures in Heaven

Lay not up for yourselves treasures upon earth, where moth and rust doth corrupt, and where thieves break through and steal:

But lay up for yourselves treasures in heaven, where neither moth nor rust doth corrupt, and where thieves do not break through nor steal:

For where your treasure is, there will your heart be also.

The light of the body is the eye: if therefore thine eye be single, thy whole body shall be full of light.

But if thine eye be evil, thy whole body shall be full of darkness. If therefore the light that is in thee be darkness, how great is that darkness!

No man can serve two masters: for either he will hate the one, and love the other; or else he will hold to the one, and despise the other. Ye cannot serve God and mammon. (Matthew 6: 19–24)

Do Not Be Anxious

Therefore I say unto you, Take no thought for your life, what ye shall eat, or what ye shall drink; nor yet for your body, what ye shall put on. Is not the life more than meat, and the body than raiment?

Behold the fowls of the air: for they sow not, neither do they reap, nor gather into barns; yet your heavenly Father feedeth them. Are ye not much better than they?

Which of you by taking thought can add one cubit unto his stature?

And why take ye thought for raiment? Consider the lilies of the field, how they grow; they toil not, neither do they spin:

And yet I say unto you, That even Solomon in all his glory was not arrayed like one of these.

Wherefore, if God so clothe the grass of the field, which to day is, and to morrow is cast into the oven, shall he not much more clothe you, O ye of little faith?

Therefore take no thought, saying, What shall we eat? or, What shall we drink? or, Wherewithal shall we be clothed?

(For after all these things do the Gentiles seek:) for your heavenly Father knoweth that ye have need of all these things.

But seek ye first the kingdom of God, and his righteousness; and all these things shall be added unto you.

Take therefore no thought for the morrow: for the morrow shall take thought for the things of itself. Sufficient unto the day is the evil thereof. (Matthew 6:25–34)

Judging Others

Judge not, that ye be not judged.

For with what judgment ye judge, ye shall be judged: and with what measure ye mete, it shall be measured to you again.

And why beholdest thou the mote that is in thy brother's eye, but considerest not the beam that is in thine own eye?

Or how wilt thou say to thy brother, Let me pull out the mote out of thine eye; and, behold, a beam is in thine own eye?

Thou hypocrite, first cast out the beam out of thine own eye; and then shalt thou see clearly to cast out the mote out of thy brother's eye.

Give not that which is holy unto the dogs, neither cast ye your pearls before swine, lest they trample them under their feet, and turn again and rend you. (Matthew 7:1–6)

Ask and It Will Be Given

Ask, and it shall be given you; seek, and ye shall find; knock, and it shall be opened unto you:

For every one that asketh receiveth; and he that seeketh findeth; and to him that knocketh it shall be opened.

Or what man is there of you, whom if his son ask bread, will he give him a stone?

Or if he ask a fish, will he give him a serpent?

If ye then, being evil, know how to give good gifts unto your children, how much more shall your Father which is in heaven give good things to them that ask him? (Matthew 7:7–11)

The Golden Rule

Therefore all things whatsoever ye would that men should do to you, do ye even so to them: for this is the law and the prophets.

Enter ye in at the strait gate: for wide is the gate, and broad is the way, that leadeth to destruction, and many there be which go in thereat:

Because strait is the gate, and narrow is the way, which leadeth unto life, and few there be that find it. (Matthew 7:12–14)

A Tree and Its Fruit

Beware of false prophets, which come to you in sheep's clothing, but inwardly they are ravening wolves.

Ye shall know them by their fruits. Do men gather grapes of thorns, or figs of thistles?

Even so every good tree bringeth forth good fruit; but a corrupt tree bringeth forth evil fruit.

A good tree cannot bring forth evil fruit, neither can a corrupt tree bring forth good fruit.

Every tree that bringeth not forth good fruit is hewn down, and cast into the fire.

Wherefore by their fruits ye shall know them. (Matthew 7:15–20)

I Never Knew You

> Not every one that saith unto me, Lord, Lord, shall enter into the kingdom of heaven; but he that doeth the will of my Father which is in heaven.

> Many will say to me in that day, Lord, Lord, have we not prophesied in thy name? and in thy name have cast out devils? and in thy name done many wonderful works?

> And then will I profess unto them, I never knew you: depart from me, ye that work iniquity. (Matthew 7:21–23)

Build Your House on the Rock

> Therefore whosoever heareth these sayings of mine, and doeth them, I will liken him unto a wise man, which built his house upon a rock:

> And the rain descended, and the floods came, and the winds blew, and beat upon that house; and it fell not: for it was founded upon a rock.

> And every one that heareth these sayings of mine, and doeth them not, shall be likened unto a foolish man, which built his house upon the sand:

> And the rain descended, and the floods came, and the winds blew, and beat upon that house; and it fell: and great was the fall of it. (Matthew 7:24–27)

The Authority of Jesus

> And it came to pass, when Jesus had ended these sayings, the people were astonished at his doctrine:

For he taught them as one having authority, and not as the scribes. (Matthew 7:28–29)

Jesus continued with His numerous miracles, signs, and wonders leading up to the Last Supper, beginning with His triumphal entry into Jerusalem and His Passover with the disciples.

Jesus Triumphal Entry into Jerusalem

And when they drew nigh unto Jerusalem, and were come to Bethphage, unto the mount of Olives, then sent Jesus two disciples,

Saying unto them, Go into the village over against you, and straightway ye shall find an ass tied, and a colt with her: loose them, and bring them unto me.

And if any man say ought unto you, ye shall say, The Lord hath need of them; and straightway he will send them.

All this was done, that it might be fulfilled which was spoken by the prophet, saying,

Tell ye the daughter of Sion, Behold, thy King cometh unto thee, meek, and sitting upon an ass, and a colt the foal of an ass.

And the disciples went, and did as Jesus commanded them,

And brought the ass, and the colt, and put on them their clothes, and they set him thereon.

And a very great multitude spread their garments in the way; others cut down branches from the trees, and strawed them in the way.

And the multitudes that went before, and that followed, cried, saying, Hosanna to the son of David: Blessed is he that cometh in the name of the Lord; Hosanna in the highest.

And when he was come into Jerusalem, all the city was moved, saying, Who is this?

And the multitude said, This is Jesus the prophet of Nazareth of Galilee. (Matthew 21:1–11)

Jesus Passover with the Disciples

Now the first day of the feast of unleavened bread the disciples came to Jesus, saying unto him, Where wilt thou that we prepare for thee to eat the passover?

And he said, Go into the city to such a man, and say unto him, The Master saith, My time is at hand; I will keep the passover at thy house with my disciples.

And the disciples did as Jesus had appointed them; and they made ready the passover.

Now when the even was come, he sat down with the twelve.

And as they did eat, he said, Verily I say unto you, that one of you shall betray me.

And they were exceeding sorrowful, and began every one of them to say unto him, Lord, is it I?

And he answered and said, He that dippeth his hand with me in the dish, the same shall betray me.

The Son of man goeth as it is written of him: but woe unto that man by whom the Son of man is betrayed! it had been good for that man if he had not been born.

Then Judas, which betrayed him, answered and said, Master, is it I? He said unto him, Thou hast said. (Matthew 26:17–25)

The Passover

"Passover or Pesach is a major Jewish holiday and one of the most widely celebrated Jewish holidays.

Passover was one of the Three Pilgrimage Festivals during which the entire population of the kingdom of Judah made a pilgrimage to the Temple in Jerusalem.[

Samaritans still make this pilgrimage to Mount Gerizim, but only men participate in public worship.

During the existence of the Temple in Jerusalem, Passover was a spring festival that was connected to the offering of the "first fruits of the barley," as barley was the first grain to ripen and to be harvested in the Land of Israel. The festivals now associated with the Exodus (Passover, Shavuot, and Sukkot) began as agricultural and seasonal feasts but became completely subsumed into the central narrative of Israel's deliverance from oppression at the hands of God.

In the Book of Exodus, God helped the Israelites escape from slavery in ancient Egypt by inflicting ten plagues upon the Egyptians before the Pharaoh would release the Israelite slaves. The last of the plagues was the death of the Egyptian first-born. The Israelites were instructed to mark the doorposts of their homes with the blood of a slaughtered spring lamb and, upon seeing this, the spirit of the Lord knew to pass over the first-born in these homes, hence the English name of the holiday.

Passover commences on the 15th of the Hebrew month of Nisan and lasts for either seven days (in Israel and for Reform Jews and other progressive Jews around the world who adhere to the biblical commandment) or eight days for Orthodox, Hasidic, and most Conservative Jews (in the diaspora). The rituals unique to the Passover celebrations commence with the Passover Seder when the 15th of Nisan has begun."[1]

---

[1] Source: en.wikipedia.org

The Last Supper

"The Last Supper is the final meal, in the Gospel accounts, that Jesus shared with his apostles in Jerusalem before his crucifixion. The Last Supper provides the scriptural basis for the Eucharist, also known as Holy Communion or The Lord's Supper.

First Corinthians contains the earliest known mention of the Last Supper. The four Gospels all state that the Last Supper took place toward the end of the week, after Jesus's triumphal entry into Jerusalem, and that Jesus and His apostles shared a meal shortly before Jesus was crucified at the end of that week.

During the meal, Jesus predicts His betrayal by one of the apostles present, and He foretells that before the next morning, Peter will deny knowing him.

The three Synoptic Gospels and 1 Corinthians include the account of the institution of the bread and wine in which Jesus takes bread, breaks it, and gives it to the apostles, saying, "This is my body which is given for you."

The Gospel of John does not include this episode but tells of Jesus washing the feet of the apostles, giving the new commandment "to love one another as I have loved you," and it has a detailed farewell discourse by Jesus, calling the apostles who follow his teachings "friends and not servants" as He prepares them for His departure.

The Last Supper served the dual purpose of venerating Passover, the escape of the Jews from slavery in Egypt, and the establishment of a new religion, Christianity."[1]

---

[1] Source: en.wikipedia.org The Last Supper Wikipedia

Scriptures on the Last Supper

And as they were eating, Jesus took bread, and blessed it, and brake it, and gave it to the disciples, and said, Take, eat; this is my body.

And he took the cup, and gave thanks, and gave it to them, saying, Drink ye all of it;

For this is my blood of the new testament, which is shed for many for the remission of sins.

But I say unto you, I will not drink henceforth of this fruit of the vine, until that day when I drink it new with you in my Father's kingdom. (Matthew 26:26–29)

And as they did eat, Jesus took bread, and blessed, and brake it, and gave to them, and said, Take, eat: this is my body.

And he took the cup, and when he had given thanks, he gave it to them: and they all drank of it.

And he said unto them, This is my blood of the new testament, which is shed for many.

Verily I say unto you, I will drink no more of the fruit of the vine, until that day that I drink it new in the kingdom of God. (Mark 14:22–24)

Then came the day of unleavened bread, when the passover must be killed.

And he sent Peter and John, saying, Go and prepare us the passover, that we may eat.

And they said unto him, Where wilt thou that we prepare?

And he said unto them, Behold, when ye are entered into the city, there shall a man meet you, bearing a pitcher of water; follow him into the house where he entereth in.

And ye shall say unto the goodman of the house, The Master saith unto thee, Where is the guestchamber, where I shall eat the passover with my disciples?

And he shall shew you a large upper room furnished: there make ready.

And they went, and found as he had said unto them: and they made ready the passover.

And when the hour was come, he sat down, and the twelve apostles with him.

And he said unto them, With desire I have desired to eat this passover with you before I suffer:

For I say unto you, I will not any more eat thereof, until it be fulfilled in the kingdom of God.

And he took the cup, and gave thanks, and said, Take this, and divide it among yourselves:

For I say unto you, I will not drink of the fruit of the vine, until the kingdom of God shall come.

And he took bread, and gave thanks, and brake it, and gave unto them, saying, This is my body which is given for you: this do in remembrance of me.

Likewise also the cup after supper, saying, This cup is the new testament in my blood, which is shed for you. (Luke 22:7–20)

CHAPTER 4

Jesus's Betrayal

Then one of the twelve, called Judas Iscariot, went unto the chief priests,

And said unto them, What will ye give me, and I will deliver him unto you? And they covenanted with him for thirty pieces of silver.

And from that time he sought opportunity to betray him. (Matthew 26:14–16)

Jesus knew who His betrayer was from the very beginning of His ministry.

But there are some of you that believe not. For Jesus knew from the beginning who they were that believed not, and who should betray him. (John 6:64)

Then Judas, which betrayed him, answered and said, Master, is it I? He said unto him, Thou hast said. (Matthew 26:25)

And after the sop Satan entered into him. Then said Jesus unto him, That thou doest, do quickly.

Now no man at the table knew for what intent he spake
this unto him. (John 13:27–28)

He also knew that His betrayal had to take place in order for us to follow
Him and reeive eternal life.

> The Gospels suggest that Jesus foresaw (John 6:64;
> Matthew 26:25) and allowed Judas's betrayal (John
> 13:27–28).

"Moreover, there are several explanations as to why Judas betrayed Jesus.
In the earliest account, in the Gospel of Mark, when he goes to the chief
priests to betray Jesus, he is offered money as a reward, but it is not clear
that money is his motivation.

In the Gospel of Matthew account, on the other hand, he asks what they
will pay him for handing Jesus over.

In the Gospel of Luke and the Gospel of John, the devil enters into Judas,
causing him to offer to betray Jesus. The Gospel of John account has Judas
complaining that money has been spent on expensive perfumes to anoint
Jesus, which could have been spent on the poor, but adds that he was the
keeper of the apostles' purse and used to steal from it.

One suggestion has been that Judas expected Jesus to overthrow Roman
rule of Israel. In this view, Judas is a disillusioned disciple betraying Jesus
not so much because he loved money, but because he loved his country
and thought Jesus had failed it.

Another explanation is that Jesus was causing unrest likely to increase
tensions with the Roman authorities, and they thought he should be
restrained until after the Passover, when everyone had gone back home
and the commotion had died down."[1]

---

[1] **Source:** en.wikipedia.org › wiki › Judas_Iscariot
Judas Iscariot - Wikipedia

Garden of Gethsemane

After Jesus had spoken all the words in the High Priestly Prayer

> HE went forth with his disciples over the brook Cedron, where was a garden, into which he entered, and his disciples.
>
> And Judas also, which betrayed him, knew the place: for Jesus ofttimes resorted thither with his disciples. (John 18:1–2)

Jesus knew He was going to be betrayed, and this was the night it would take place. He said to His disciples to stay awake with Him because He was going to pray, and Jesus withdrew from His disciples.

> a stone's cast, and kneeled down, and prayed,
>
> Saying, Father, if thou be willing, remove this cup from me: nevertheless not my will, but thine, be done.
>
> And there appeared an angel unto him from heaven, strengthening him.
>
> And being in an agony he prayed more earnestly: and his sweat was as it were great drops of blood falling down to the ground.
>
> And when he rose up from prayer, and was come to his disciples, he found them sleeping for sorrow,
>
> And said unto them, Why sleep ye? rise and pray, lest ye enter into temptation. (Luke 22:41–46)

As Jesus was completing His conversation with His disciples, the time of His capture for His trials was taking place.

Judas then, having received a band of men and officers from the chief priests and Pharisees, cometh thither with lanterns and torches and weapons.

Jesus therefore, knowing all things that should come upon him, went forth, and said unto them, Whom seek ye?

They answered him, Jesus of Nazareth. Jesus saith unto them, I am he. And Judas also, which betrayed him, stood with them.

As soon then as he had said unto them, I am he, they went backward, and fell to the ground.

Then asked he them again, Whom seek ye? And they said, Jesus of Nazareth.

Jesus answered, I have told you that I am he: if therefore ye seek me, let these go their way:

That the saying might be fulfilled, which he spake, Of them which thou gavest me have I lost none. (John 18:3–9)

Most people, as they plot their betrayal of someone they want to have killed, have a specific place set up for the murder. Judas had a place in mind, in the Garden of Gethsemane.

Jesus Betrayed with a Kiss

Just as he was speaking, Judas, one of the Twelve, appeared. With him was a crowd armed with swords and clubs, sent from the chief priests, the teachers of the law, and the elders.

Now the betrayer had arranged a signal with them: "The one I kiss is the man; arrest him and lead him away under guard."

Going at once to Jesus, Judas said, "Rabbi!" and kissed him.

The men seized Jesus and arrested him. (Mark 14:43–46)

What is the significance of Judas betraying Jesus with a kiss? It is simply for identification. Though kisses are usually among friends, this kiss was simply for identification.

CHAPTER 5

The Trials of Jesus According to the Gospels

Whenever a believer attempts to do good for everyone, there are always people who want to destroy the good, and most of the time they are within the body of Christ. This still holds true today, as it was true when Jesus was on this earth.

The Sanhedrin Court consisting of Jewish priests took the lead to try and destroy Jesus and His purpose on earth.

"The four canonical gospels tell us how Jesus is tried and condemned by the Sanhedrin, although not all members were present. According to Luke, Joseph of Arimathea and Nicodemus dissented from these accusations.

These Jewish leaders condemned Jesus for violating the Sabbath law (by healing on the Sabbath), threatening to destroy the Jewish Temple, sorcery, exorcising people by the power of demons, and claiming to be both the Messiah and the Son of God. During all of these accusations, Jesus was generally quiet, did not mount a defense, and rarely responds to these accusations.

Although the Gospel accounts vary with respect to some of the details, they agree on the general character and overall structure of the trials of Jesus."[1]

Trials	Matthew	Mark	Luke	John	Verdict
Sanhedrin	26:57–67	14:53–65	22:54, 66–71		Guilty of death
Annas				John 18:12, 13, 19, 24	Guilty of death
Pilate	27:1–2, 11–26	15:1–15	23:1–6	18:29–39 19:1–16	Guilty only because of his fear of the people
Herod			23:7–15		Not guilty

Source: https://en.wikipedia.org/wiki/Sanhedrin_trial_of_Jesus

I hope these trials of Jesus Christ were amazing to you as they were to me. You have seen how we, the body of Christ, can be more accusatory than unbelievers, causing the innocent to be punished more than the guilty.

The Scriptures say in Matthew 7:1, "Judge not least ye be judged."

As the body of Christ, we should learn to love and accept each other. We should not condemn or defile anyone, his or her ministry, or the day one chooses to worship God.

We are to let the unbelievers see, know, and believe that the Scripture in John 13:35, is what we strictly adhere to.

By this shall all men know that ye are my disciples, if ye have love one to another.

This love abideth within us as we stand on these two scriptures, the greatest commandments in Mark 12.

And thou shalt love the Lord thy God with all thy heart,
and with all thy soul, and with all thy mind, and with all
thy strength: this is the first commandment.

And the second is like, namely this, Thou shalt love thy
neighbour as thyself. There is none other commandment
greater than these. (Mark 12:30–31)

Love is a very powerful tool and draws you to the person, not deflecting
you away. God's love for you drew you to Him, and therefore when the
love you have for one another is effective in you, others can see it and want
to become a part of what they see in you.

First Corinthians 13 goes even further in sharing with us about love.

Though I speak with the tongues of men and of angels,
and have not charity, I am become as sounding brass, or
a tinkling cymbal.

And though I have the gift of prophecy, and understand
all mysteries, and all knowledge; and though I have all
faith, so that I could remove mountains, and have not
charity, I am nothing.

And though I bestow all my goods to feed the poor, and
though I give my body to be burned, and have not charity,
it profiteth me nothing.

Charity suffereth long, and is kind; charity envieth not;
charity vaunteth not itself, is not puffed up,

Doth not behave itself unseemly, seeketh not her own, is
not easily provoked, thinketh no evil;

Rejoiceth not in iniquity, but rejoiceth in the truth;

Beareth all things, believeth all things, hopeth all things, endureth all things.

Charity never faileth: but whether there be prophecies, they shall fail; whether there be tongues, they shall cease; whether there be knowledge, it shall vanish away.

And now abideth faith, hope, charity, these three; but the greatest of these is charity. (1 Corinthians 13:1–8, 13)

Show the love of God in your lives and see the difference it makes.

CHAPTER 6

Jesus's Crucifixion

"The crucifixion of Jesus occurred in first century Judea, most probably between the years AD 30 and 33.

According to the gospels, Jesus Christ, was arrested, tried, and sentenced by Pontius Pilate, to be scourged and finally crucified by the Romans. Jesus was stripped of His clothing and offered wine mixed with gall to drink before being crucified. He was then hung between two convicted thieves and died some six hours later." [1]

During this time, the soldiers affixed a sign to the top of the cross stating, "Jesus of Nazareth, King of the Jews," in three languages, Hebrew, Latin, and Greek (John 19:20).

Scriptures on Jesus Crucifixion:

> Then Pilate therefore took Jesus, and scourged him.
>
> And the soldiers platted a crown of thorns, and put it on his head, and they put on him a purple robe,
>
> And said, Hail, King of the Jews! and they smote him with their hands.

---

[1] source: https://en.wikipedia.org/wiki/Crucifixion_of_Jesus

Pilate therefore went forth again, and saith unto them, Behold, I bring him forth to you, that ye may know that I find no fault in him.

Then came Jesus forth, wearing the crown of thorns, and the purple robe. And Pilate saith unto them, Behold the man!

When the chief priests therefore and officers saw him, they cried out, saying, Crucify him, crucify him. Pilate saith unto them, Take ye him, and crucify him: for I find no fault in him.

The Jews answered him, We have a law, and by our law he ought to die, because he made himself the Son of God.

When Pilate therefore heard that saying, he was the more afraid;

And went again into the judgment hall, and saith unto Jesus, Whence art thou? But Jesus gave him no answer.

Then saith Pilate unto him, Speakest thou not unto me? knowest thou not that I have power to crucify thee, and have power to release thee?

Jesus answered, Thou couldest have no power at all against me, except it were given thee from above: therefore he that delivered me unto thee hath the greater sin.

And from thenceforth Pilate sought to release him: but the Jews cried out, saying, If thou let this man go, thou art not Caesar's friend: whosoever maketh himself a king speaketh against Caesar.

When Pilate therefore heard that saying, he brought Jesus forth, and sat down in the judgment seat in a place that is called the Pavement, but in the Hebrew, Gabbatha.

And it was the preparation of the passover, and about the sixth hour: and he saith unto the Jews, Behold your King!

But they cried out, Away with him, away with him, crucify him. Pilate saith unto them, Shall I crucify your King? The chief priests answered, We have no king but Caesar.

Then delivered he him therefore unto them to be crucified. And they took Jesus, and led him away.

And he bearing his cross went forth into a place called the place of a skull, which is called in the Hebrew Golgotha:

Where they crucified him, and two other with him, on either side one, and Jesus in the midst.

And Pilate wrote a title, and put it on the cross. And the writing was Jesus **OF NAZARETH THE KING OF THE JEWS**.

This title then read many of the Jews: for the place where Jesus was crucified was nigh to the city: and it was written in Hebrew, and Greek, and Latin.

Then said the chief priests of the Jews to Pilate, Write not, The King of the Jews; but that he said, I am King of the Jews.

Pilate answered, What I have written I have written.

Then the soldiers, when they had crucified Jesus, took his garments, and made four parts, to every soldier a part; and also his coat: now the coat was without seam, woven from the top throughout.

They said therefore among themselves, Let us not rend it, but cast lots for it, whose it shall be: that the scripture might be fulfilled, which saith, They parted my raiment among them, and for my vesture they did cast lots. These things therefore the soldiers did.

Now there stood by the cross of Jesus his mother, and his mother's sister, Mary the wife of Cleophas, and Mary Magdalene.

When Jesus therefore saw his mother, and the disciple standing by, whom he loved, he saith unto his mother, Woman, behold thy son!

Then saith he to the disciple, Behold thy mother! And from that hour that disciple took her unto his own home.

After this, Jesus knowing that all things were now accomplished, that the scripture might be fulfilled, saith, I thirst.

Now there was set a vessel full of vinegar: and they filled a spunge with vinegar, and put it upon hyssop, and put it to his mouth.

When Jesus therefore had received the vinegar, he said, It is finished: and he bowed his head, and gave up the ghost.

The Jews therefore, because it was the preparation, that the bodies should not remain upon the cross on the sabbath day, (for that sabbath day was an high day,) besought Pilate that their legs might be broken, and that they might be taken away.

Then came the soldiers, and brake the legs of the first, and of the other which was crucified with him.

But when they came to Jesus, and saw that he was dead already, they brake not his legs:

But one of the soldiers with a spear pierced his side, and forthwith came there out blood and water.

And he that saw it bare record, and his record is true: and he knoweth that he saith true, that ye might believe.

For these things were done, that the scripture should be fulfilled, A bone of him shall not be broken.

And again another scripture saith, They shall look on him whom they pierced.

And after this Joseph of Arimathaea, being a disciple of Jesus, but secretly for fear of the Jews, besought Pilate that he might take away the body of Jesus: and Pilate gave him leave. He came therefore, and took the body of Jesus.

And there came also Nicodemus, which at the first came to Jesus by night, and brought a mixture of myrrh and aloes, about an hundred pound weight.

Then took they the body of Jesus, and wound it in linen clothes with the spices, as the manner of the Jews is to bury.

Now in the place where he was crucified there was a garden; and in the garden a new sepulchre, wherein was never man yet laid.

There laid they Jesus therefore because of the Jews' preparation day; for the sepulchre was nigh at hand. (John 19:1–42)

"The Seven Last Phrases of Jesus

1. Father, forgive them, for they know not what they do. (Luke 23:34)
2. Today you will be with me in paradise. (Luke 23:43)
3. Behold thy son: behold thy mother. (John 19:26–27)
4. My God, my God, why hast thou forsaken me? (Mark 15:34)
5. I thirst. (John 19:28)
6. It is finished. (John 19:30)
7. Father, into thy hands I commend my spirit. (Luke 23:46)"[2]

---

[2] en.wikipedia.org › wiki › Sayings_of_Jesus_on_the_cross

Supernatural Events That Occurred during Jesus Crucifixion

Now from the sixth hour there was darkness over all the land unto the ninth hour.

And about the ninth hour Jesus cried with a loud voice, saying, Eli, Eli, lama sabachthani? that is to say, My God, my God, why hast thou forsaken me?

Some of them that stood there, when they heard that, said, This man calleth for Elias.

And straightway one of them ran, and took a spunge, and filled it with vinegar, and put it on a reed, and gave him to drink.

The rest said, Let be, let us see whether Elias will come to save him.

Jesus, when he had cried again with a loud voice, yielded up the ghost.

And, behold, the veil of the temple was rent in twain from the top to the bottom; and the earth did quake, and the rocks rent;

And the graves were opened; and many bodies of the saints which slept arose. (Matthew 27:45–52)

CHAPTER 7

Jesus's Resurrection

What a glorious day this was to Jesus's followers to know the words He had spoken regarding His resurrection had truly come to pass.

> From that time forth began Jesus to shew unto his disciples, how that he must go unto Jerusalem, and suffer many things of the elders and chief priests and scribes, and be killed, and be raised again the third day.

> Then Peter took him, and began to rebuke him, saying, Be it far from thee, Lord: this shall not be unto thee.

> But he turned, and said unto Peter, Get thee behind me, Satan: thou art an offence unto me: for thou savourest not the things that be of God, but those that be of men.

> Then said Jesus unto his disciples, If any man will come after me, let him deny himself, and take up his cross, and follow me.

> For whosoever will save his life shall lose it: and whosoever will lose his life for my sake shall find it.

> For what is a man profited, if he shall gain the whole world, and lose his own soul? or what shall a man give in exchange for his soul?

For the Son of man shall come in the glory of his Father with his angels; and then he shall reward every man according to his works.

Verily I say unto you, There be some standing here, which shall not taste of death, till they see the Son of man coming in his kingdom. (Matthew 16:21–28)

And while they abode in Galilee, Jesus said unto them, The Son of man shall be betrayed into the hands of men:

And they shall kill him, and the third day he shall be raised again. And they were exceeding sorry. (Matthew 17:22–23)

And Jesus going up to Jerusalem took the twelve disciples apart in the way, and said unto them,

Behold, we go up to Jerusalem; and the Son of man shall be betrayed unto the chief priests and unto the scribes, and they shall condemn him to death,

And shall deliver him to the Gentiles to mock, and to scourge, and to crucify him: and the third day he shall rise again. (Matthew 20:17–19)

Saying, The Son of man must suffer many things, and be rejected of the elders and chief priests and scribes, and be slain, and be raised the third day.

And he said to them all, If any man will come after me, let him deny himself, and take up his cross daily, and follow me.

For whosoever will save his life shall lose it: but whosoever will lose his life for my sake, the same shall save it.

For what is a man advantaged, if he gain the whole world, and lose himself, or be cast away?

For whosoever shall be ashamed of me and of my words, of him shall the Son of man be ashamed, when he shall come in his own glory, and in his Father's, and of the holy angels.

But I tell you of a truth, there be some standing here, which shall not taste of death, till they see the kingdom of God. (Luke 9:22–27)

And they departed thence, and passed through Galilee; and he would not that any man should know it.

For he taught his disciples, and said unto them, The Son of man is delivered into the hands of men, and they shall kill him; and after that he is killed, he shall rise the third day.

But they understood not that saying, and were afraid to ask him. (Mark 9:30–32)

This was the awesome day revealed to Jesus's followers and others. Jesus truly rose again.

The first day of the week cometh Mary Magdalene early, when it was yet dark, unto the sepulchre, and seeth the stone taken away from the sepulchre.

Then she runneth, and cometh to Simon Peter, and to the other disciple, whom Jesus loved, and saith unto them, They have taken away the LORD out of the sepulchre, and we know not where they have laid him.

Peter therefore went forth, and that other disciple, and came to the sepulchre.

So they ran both together: and the other disciple did outrun Peter, and came first to the sepulchre.

And he stooping down, and looking in, saw the linen clothes lying; yet went he not in.

Then cometh Simon Peter following him, and went into the sepulchre, and seeth the linen clothes lie,

And the napkin, that was about his head, not lying with the linen clothes, but wrapped together in a place by itself.

Then went in also that other disciple, which came first to the sepulchre, and he saw, and believed.

For as yet they knew not the scripture, that he must rise again from the dead.

Then the disciples went away again unto their own home.

But Mary stood without at the sepulchre weeping: and as she wept, she stooped down, and looked into the sepulchre,

And seeth two angels in white sitting, the one at the head, and the other at the feet, where the body of Jesus had lain.

And they say unto her, Woman, why weepest thou? She saith unto them, Because they have taken away my LORD, and I know not where they have laid him.

And when she had thus said, she turned herself back, and saw Jesus standing, and knew not that it was Jesus.

Jesus saith unto her, Woman, why weepest thou? whom seekest thou? She, supposing him to be the gardener, saith unto him, Sir, if thou have borne him hence, tell me where thou hast laid him, and I will take him away.

Jesus saith unto her, Mary. She turned herself, and saith unto him, Rabboni; which is to say, Master.

Jesus saith unto her, Touch me not; for I am not yet ascended to my Father: but go to my brethren, and say unto them, I ascend unto my Father, and your Father; and to my God, and your God.

Mary Magdalene came and told the disciples that she had seen the LORD, and that he had spoken these things unto her.

Then the same day at evening, being the first day of the week, when the doors were shut where the disciples were assembled for fear of the Jews, came Jesus and stood in the midst, and saith unto them, Peace be unto you.

And when he had so said, he shewed unto them his hands and his side. Then were the disciples glad, when they saw the LORD.

Then said Jesus to them again, Peace be unto you: as my Father hath sent me, even so send I you.

22 And when he had said this, he breathed on them, and saith unto them, Receive ye the Holy Ghost:

Whose soever sins ye remit, they are remitted unto them; and whose soever sins ye retain, they are retained.

But Thomas, one of the twelve, called Didymus, was not with them when Jesus came.

The other disciples therefore said unto him, We have seen the LORD. But he said unto them, Except I shall see in his hands the print of the nails, and put my finger into the print of the nails, and thrust my hand into his side, I will not believe.

And after eight days again his disciples were within, and Thomas with them: then came Jesus, the doors being shut, and stood in the midst, and said, Peace be unto you.

Then saith he to Thomas, Reach hither thy finger, and behold my hands; and reach hither thy hand, and thrust it into my side: and be not faithless, but believing.

And Thomas answered and said unto him, My LORD and my God.

Jesus saith unto him, Thomas, because thou hast seen me, thou hast believed: blessed are they that have not seen, and yet have believed.

And many other signs truly did Jesus in the presence of his disciples, which are not written in this book:

But these are written, that ye might believe that Jesus is the Christ, the Son of God; and that believing ye might have life through his name. (John 20:1–31)

CHAPTER 8

Jesus's Ascension

Isn't it a wonderful, marvelous, and exhilarating feeling to know that when Jesus returns, we are going to be caught up with him in the clouds, forever to be with Jesus.in heaven.

What a day it is going to be, when everything foretold in the Bible regarding Jesus's return is going to be manifested. Hallelujah, Hallelujah, Hallelujah.

> And, being assembled together with them, commanded them that they should not depart from Jerusalem, but wait for the promise of the Father, which, saith he, ye have heard of me.

> For John truly baptized with water; but ye shall be baptized with the Holy Ghost not many days hence.

> When they therefore were come together, they asked of him, saying, Lord, wilt thou at this time restore again the kingdom to Israel?

> And he said unto them, It is not for you to know the times or the seasons, which the Father hath put in his own power.

But ye shall receive power, after that the Holy Ghost is come upon you: and ye shall be witnesses unto me both in Jerusalem, and in all Judaea, and in Samaria, and unto the uttermost part of the earth.

And when he had spoken these things, while they beheld, he was taken up; and a cloud received him out of their sight.

And while they looked stedfastly toward heaven as he went up, behold, two men stood by them in white apparel;

Which also said, Ye men of Galilee, why stand ye gazing up into heaven? this same Jesus, which is taken up from you into heaven, shall so come in like manner as ye have seen him go into heaven. (Acts 1:4–11)

I truly hope, pray, and believe this book has changed, awakened, and renewed those who have read it to the extent they have been revitalized, energized, and spiritualized and want to share this book with their friends, relatives, coworkers, and others so they too can know the journey of Jesus and His disciples and what their ultimate reward is, reigning with JESUS eternally.

When we as disciples of Jesus come into the realization of who we are, whom we belong to, and what our purpose is on this earth, we can see how we can change the world.

Thank you,

Pastor Revella Booker Pugh

BIBLIOGRAPHY

Introduction
Website ©2020 AV1611.com King James Dictionary DUC

Chapter 1
en.wikipedia.org Biblical Magi – Wikipedia
https://en.wikipedia.org/wiki/Miracles_of_Jesus
en.wikipedia.org wiki Decapolis
www.biblestudy.org

Chapter 2
https://en.wikipedia.org/wiki/Andrew_the_Apostle
https://en.wikipedia.org/wiki/Bartholomew_the_Apostle
en.wikipedia.org, James the Great – Wikipedia
britanica.com Saint James
APOSTLE, SON OF ZEBEDEE
WRITTEN BY: 2

• The Editors of Encyclopaedia Britannica
LAST UPDATED Jan 1, 2020 See Article History
en.wikipedia.org/wiki/
biblehub.com, Smith's Bible Dictionary James the Less
: https://en.wikipedia.org/wiki/John_the_Apostle
britanica.com, St. John the Apostle
CHRISTIAN APOSTLE
WRITTEN BY: Henry Chadwick
See Article History

https://en.wikipedia.org/wiki/John_the_Apostle

CITATION:
www.en.wikipedia.org/wiki/Sacred_tradition

https://en.wikipedia.org/wiki/John_the_Apostle

en.wikipedia.org › wiki › Myrrhbearers

https://en.wikipedia.org/wiki/John_the_Apostle

en.wikipedia.org › wiki › Disciple_whom_Jesus_loved
: https://en.wikipedia.org/wiki/Judas_Iscariot
en.wikipedia.org › wiki › Jude_the_Apostle
http://projects.mcah.columbia.edu/medieval-architecture/htm/sw/ma_
sw_gloss_matthew.htm
Source: Saint Matthew the Apostle
September 211
from *The Golden Legend*
en.wikipedia.org, Matthew the Apostle, Wikipedia
www.en.wikipedia.org, St. Peter Wikipedia
en.wikipedia.org, Philip, The Apostle Wikipedia
wikipedia.com, Simon the Zealot, Wikipedia
britannica.com, Saint Simon the Apostle
CHRISTIAN APOSTLE
WRITTEN BY: The Editors of Encyclopaedia Britannica
See Article History
britanica.com, St. Thomas
CHRISTIAN APOSTLE
WRITTEN BY: The Editors of Encyclopaedia Britannica
LAST UPDATED: Jan 1, 2020 See Article History

Chapter 3
en.wikipedia.org
en.wikipedia.org The Last Supper Wikipedia

Chapter 5
en.wikipedia.org › wiki › Judas_Iscariot
https://en.wikipedia.org/wiki/Sanhedrin_trial_of_Jesus

Chapter 6
https://en.wikipedia.org/wiki/Crucifixion_of_Jesus
en.wikipedia.org › wiki › Sayings_of_Jesus_on_the_cross

All Bible scriptures are from the King James Version.

JESUS AND THE DISCIPLES JOURNEY

Pastor Revella Booker Pugh

BIOGRAPHY

Pastor Revella Booker Pugh is the Shepherd at GOD'S ANOINTED HOUSE in Highland Heights, OH.

Pastor Pugh was born in Clarksdale, Ms. to Steve and Louetta Booker and was the youngest of 22 brothers and sisters. Her father died at an early age, leaving her mother to take care of the family.

Many times her family did not have enough food, shelter or clothing, but GOD always provided. Pastor Pugh truly believes this was the beginning of her journey to being a disciple of Jesus Christ.

Pastor Pugh has two beautiful children, Bethany Lynne Pugh and Lorenzo Pugh, Jr. whom she trained to be disciples of Jesus Christ.

Humble beginnings served as God's training, calling Pastor Pugh into shepherding GOD'S ANOINTED HOUSE. GOD revealed to Pastor

Pugh that He does not call the qualified, but qualifies the called. He showed Pastor Pugh great and mighty things she knew not.

With God's leading, Pastor Pugh first ministered to the homeless and hungry. Having experienced the same in her own life, God knew she was hungry to feed these souls for JESUS. Many homeless and hungry souls were brought to JESUS. Pastor Pugh received the Rose Palfy Award in recognition for these ministry missions, from Front Steps Housing and Services.

Pastor Pugh disciples in many other areas such as: The Adopted School Program in Cleveland, Oh, distribution of Christian Leadership material, Christian counseling and ministering to family and friends.

Pastor Pugh is the President of the Board of Trustees at GOD'S ANOINTED HOUSE in Highland Heights and serves in the community.

Pastor Pugh gives GOD all the praise and all the glory for the life He has given her.

Printed in the United States
By Bookmasters